Movement in Two Dimensions

OLIVE COOK

Movement in Two Dimensions

*A study of the animated and projected pictures
which preceded the invention of cinematography*

HUTCHINSON OF LONDON

HUTCHINSON & CO. (*Publishers*) LTD
178–202 Great Portland Street, London, W.1

London Melbourne Sydney
Auckland Bombay Toronto
Johannesburg New York

First published 1963

*This book has been set in Bembo type face. It has
been printed in Great Britain by The Anchor Press,
Ltd., in Tiptree, Essex, on Antique Wove paper.*

Acknowledgements

My thanks are due first and foremost to Mr. John and Mr. William Barnes, whose collection forms the recently opened Museum of Cinematography at St. Ives, for introducing me to the subject of this book and for giving me access to their unique collection of optic toys; and to my husband Edwin Smith for his enthusiastic support and for taking most of the photographs in the book. I am also much indebted to Mr. George Speaight for general information about shadow plays, as well as for giving a wonderful performance with the Javanese shades in his possession; to Mr. S. Esin of Istanbul for details about the Turkish shadow theatre; and to Mr. Nicholas Yalouris for making arrangements for the photographs of the Xapidhamos shadow show to be taken. I am grateful, too, to Mr. Hermann Hecht for showing me some of the early hand-painted slides in his fine collection. I also wish to thank the directors of the Walker Art Gallery, Liverpool, and the Science Museum and the National Gallery, London, for allowing me to reproduce work in those collections. And, finally, I have had invaluable help from my kind publishers; in particular, Mr. Jonathan Price.

Contents

1   Mirrors and Magic   11

2   Peepshows and Panoramas   23

3   Far Eastern Shadows   47

4   Karagöz   59

5   The Chinese Shades   67

6   Dissolving Views   81

7   Living Models   101

8   The Persistence of Vision   121

    Bibliography   137

    Index   139

Illustrations

Frontispiece Excelsior—a Victorian slide from life models

Optic toys   *facing page* 20

Phantasmagoria lanternist at work   21

Magic mirrors   28

Peepshow at Bartholomew Fair, and Hoog-
    straaten's perspective box   29

Two views of the Place Vendôme peepshow   36

Daguerre's dioramas   37

Diorama playbill   44

The Regent's Park Diorama   45

Moving-picture book   52

Hand shadows   53

Oriental shadow puppets   60

Turkish shadow puppets   61

Greek shadow-play booth   68

Scenes from a Greek shadow play   69

ILLUSTRATIONS

Early panoramic slides   *facing page* 76

Lanterns, a lanternist, and his programme   77

Hand-painted slides and a rocking slide   84

Victorian slides from life models   85, 92, 93, 116

Thaumatrope discs   117

Zoetrope bands and Phenakistiscope discs   124

Projectors and photographs of movement by
    Muybridge   125

1

Mirrors and Magic

What is this
That rises like the issue of a king?
SHAKESPEARE

A SHOWMAN IN Ben Jonson's *Bartholomew Fair*, who styles himself 'Master of the Motions', gives a performance with puppets of *The ancient modern History of Hero and Leander*. 'Do you play it according to the printed Book?' he is asked, and replies: 'By no means, Sir. . . . A better way, Sir, that is too learned and poetical for our Audience: What, do they know what Hellespont is? guilty of true Love's Blood? or what *Abidos* is? or the other, *Sestos* height?' 'Th'art i' the right,' rejoins the other, adding, although he is a gentleman from Harrow who claims to have read the book in question: 'I do not know myself.' The showman goes on to say: 'I have only made it a little easie and modern for the Times, Sir, that's all. As for the Hellespont, I imagine our Thames here; and then Leander I make a Dyer's son about Puddle-Wharf, and Hero a wench o' the Bank-side, who going over one morning to Old Fish Street Leander spies her land at Trig Stairs, and falls in Love with her. Now do I introduce Cupid, having Metamorphos'd himself into a Drawer, and he strikes Hero in love with a Pint of Sherry.'

Not only does the word *Motions* strike a familiar note to ears attuned to the terms *motion pictures* and *movies*, but the showman's treatment of the book is paralleled by the film director's customary handling of themes adapted from novels and plays. Millions of cinema-goers enjoyed such films as *War and Peace* or *Henry V* who would never have dreamed of reading the original text, and if

II

there were others who had glanced at the books they would have had either to read with as little understanding as Bartholomew Cokes in Ben Jonson's comedy or to recognize and accept the essential character of the cinema to derive real pleasure from the performances. Like the motion at the Fair, the moving picture is a popular entertainment. Despite all attempts to make it ape the theatre, the film always relies for its most spectacular successes not on psychological conflict, nor upon subtle interpretations of the tragi-comic implications of the human situation, but upon visual effects which thrill and astonish, upon magical illusions which make little or no demand on the intelligence. The film can conjure up a lunar landscape, as seemingly authentic as the view we see each day from our own windows; it can reveal in every detail the mysteries of the deepest ocean bed; can transport us to other ages—to ancient Babylon, to the field of Agincourt or to Moscow going up in flames in 1812. The magic screen shows us corpses springing to life and spirits rising from their graves, it evokes a fantasy world where divers leave the swimming bath feet first and sail gracefully through the air to alight on the end of the diving-board, and a bowler-hatted hero grows substantial wings and hovers above the streets of his native slum.

We all know that there is nothing supernatural about the production of these marvels. But when we are actually in front of the screen very few of us think of the science and apparatus which have gone to the making of the film. We succumb entirely to the convincing power of that flat screen. It seldom even occurs to us to remember that the figures we see gesticulating before us with all the semblance of life are not really moving at all, that it is only a curious property of the eye, the so-called persistence of vision, which gives them animation. We are absorbed and we are conscious, even in this sophisticated age, of a sense of magic. And this response is rooted in the history of the film, for the earliest producers of two-dimensional moving images were magicians and the whole development of the moving picture was shaped by their uncanny practices.

Like the theatre, the cinema originated in ritual, but from the beginning it exhibited characteristics which sharply differentiated it from the drama. The drama was always three-dimensional, but the actual furniture of the scenes existed only through the ability of the actors to command the spectator's imagination. They represented gods or mythical heroes and showed a developing conflict which ended in either tragedy or comedy and moved the audience to sympathetic tears or laughter. But the earliest moving pictures were, like those of today, two-dimensional spectacles; they had no substance, and their effects, far from depending upon the power of the actor, were often produced without the aid of living persons; they sought to arouse no emotions but those of astonishment, terror, and awe, and the terror they hoped to inspire was not the cathartic terror of the drama caused by participation in another's suffering, but a nightmarish terror of the unknown. For these first productions, visions summoned up by sorcerer-priests, aimed at presenting phenomena beyond the grasp of the human mind.

Pliny the Elder relates that the god Hercules would regularly show himself, gigantic in stature, among the vapours of the fire kindled in his temple at Tyre; Aesculapius often displayed himself to his worshippers at Agrigento, while the temple at Enginium, also in Sicily, was so celebrated for apparitions of the two divinities Hera and Aphrodite that the shrine became a place of seasonal pilgrimage. Iamblichus informs us that it was the priests, who were also magicians, who were responsible for these appearances, and that they were always accompanied by smoke and vapours; he describes one occasion in particular when a conjurer named Maximus produced a monstrous figure of Hecate who made an overwhelming impression on an audience already trembling with fear by laughing aloud with heaving shoulders and diabolical grimaces.

It has long since been known that these illusions were created by means of various metal mirrors, most commonly of silver. In the collection of the Barnes brothers at Mousehole there is a curious convex metallic mirror that came from Japan and was once one of the staple instruments in the cabinet of a magician. The mirror is circular and about 5 in. in diameter; it has a knob in the centre of the back by which it can be held, and on the rest of the back are circles stamped in relief with a border of Greek key design. If you look into its highly polished convex face you will see an image, more like a minutely detailed enamelled portrait than a reflection, of your own features about half their natural size. This mirror has the astonishing property that when you reflect the rays of the sun from its polished surface the image of the ornamental border and the circles stamped on the back is seen distinctly upon the wall of the room.

Sir David Brewster explains that 'the spectrum in the luminous area is not an image of the figures on the back, but the figures are a copy of the picture which the artist has drawn on the surface of the mirror and so concealed by polishing that it is invisible in ordinary light and can only be brought out by the sun's rays'. He had noticed that lines and circles were reflected by the light of the sun from polished steel buttons; these marks and rings had been made by the action of the polishing powder but were too faint to be seen by the eye.

Such mirrors, generally known as Chinese mirrors, were useful aids in producing mysterious effects, but it was the concave mirror upon which the magician depended for his most staggering results.

Its surface was elliptical, so that if any object was placed in one focus of the ellipse an inverted image of it would appear in the other focus. To a spectator rightly placed, this image would seem as if suspended in the air, and if the mirror and object were both hidden from his view the effect would take on the character of the supernatural. The difficulty of getting a living person to assume an inverted position, which must often have been necessary, was overcome by employing a second concave mirror. The size of the aerial image was in proportion to the distance of the real object from the mirror; thus by varying the distance of the object the size of the image could be increased or diminished.

It is probable that it was by means such as this that the Witch of Endor conjured up the shade of Samuel for Saul; and when the Emperor Basil of Macedonia was vouchsafed a sight of his dead son through the agency of a priest celebrated as a miracle-worker it must have been an aerial image that he saw of a painting of the boy on horseback. As the picture approached the mirror, the image advanced into the Emperor's arms, only, of course, to elude his affectionate grasp and vanish. Effects such as this have their counterparts in the modern cinema theatre, where a train or a car will rush at terrifying speed straight at the spectator.

The old Oxford tale that Friar Bacon walked between two steeples may well have originated in a deception practised with the aid of concave mirrors. And some of the wandering entertainers of the Middle Ages, those known as tregetours, produced magic spectacles which their audiences believed to be the work of the Devil, but which appear to have been contrived by mirrors. The use of concave mirrors would certainly explain the tricks of the tregetours described by Chaucer in the Franklin's Tale. Spectators seated in a hall saw a barge rowing on a sheet of water, a vine laden with black and white grapes, and a castle; and the knight Aurelius, who accompanied a tregetour to his house, was shown forests full of wild deer, falconers by the banks of a river, and knights jousting.

> 'And after this he dide hym swich pleasaunce
> That he hym shewed his lady on a daunce,
> On which hymself he daunced, as hym thoughte;
> And whan this maister that this magyk wroughte
> Saugh it was tyme, he clapte his handes two,
> And farewell! al oure revel was ago.
> And yet remoeved they never out of the hous,
> While they saugh al this sighte merveillous . . .'

From the accounts which have been transmitted of these mysterious spectacles it is evident that most of them took place either in an interior over which the priest or magician had complete control or in the open air at night, and that they were usually accompanied by fire, clouds of vapour, and the burning of incense. The impression made under such conditions upon superstitious minds can well be imagined. But some idea of how such an illusion struck a man who was far from ignorant and not easily frightened is conveyed by Cellini's celebrated account in his memoirs of his encounter with the Sicilian magician. It is perhaps significant that the magician came from Sicily, where in antiquity the temples were so specially famed for divine apparitions.

Cellini relates how he fell into conversation with a Sicilian priest, 'a man of most lofty mind, and with an excellent knowledge of Latin and Greek', and chanced to mention that he had all his life longed to see and hear something of the art of necromancy. The priest invited him to be present at a manifestation and appointed as the place of meeting the Colosseum at dead of night. Cellini was told he could bring not more than two companions with him. When they reached the Colosseum the priest drew circles on the ground, uttering incantations and burning perfumes and evil-smelling stuff. With him there was another magician in whose hands he placed the pentacle, and then they all stood within the circle while the priest began his conjuring, Cellini and his

15

friends attending the fire. An hour and a half went by and then so many spirits appeared that the Colosseum was full of them. Cellini registers neither astonishment nor fear in his description of them. 'Benvenuto, ask of them something,' said the priest. He answered, 'Let them transport me to my Sicilian Angelica.' There was no reply and the priest said Cellini must come another time, but must bring with him a young boy of 'perfect purity'.

So on a subsequent night he returned to the same place accompanied by one of the assistants from his workshop, a boy of about twelve years old, and by two friends, Vincenzio Romoli and Agnolino Gaddi. The same preparations were made as before, but this time with greater ceremony. Benvenuto held the pentacle this time, while his friends tended the fire and the burning incense. The priest then began to call by their names the princes of the demoniac legions, invoking them in Hebrew, Greek, and Latin. Very soon the whole Colosseum was full of them. Once more Cellini asked that he might be with his Angelica. The priest said, 'Do you hear what they say?—that in a month's time you will be where she is.'

The spirits seemed to number thousands and the boy who was under the pentacle trembled with fright and cried out that round them were

'a million of the most warlike men and they were threatening us. Moreover, said he, four huge giants had appeared. They were armed and they made as if they would enter our circle. At this the necromancer, who was shaking with fright, tried with all the soft and gentle words he could think of to bid them go. Vincenzio Romoli, looking after the perfumes, was quivering like a reed. But I, who was just as much afraid, forced on myself a braver mien, and inspirited them in wonderful fashion, though indeed I nearly died when I saw the magician's fright. The boy, who had put his head between his knees, said, "I'll die in this way since die we must." Then I said to the child, "These creatures are all lower than us, and what you see is only smoke and shade; so lift up your eyes." When he had done so he spoke once more. "The whole Colosseum is on fire and the fire is upon us," and putting his hand to his face again he said he was dead and he would not look any more. The necromancer entreated me to stand by him, also to make fumes of assafoetida. So turning to Vincenzio Romoli I told him to do this, and looked at Agnolino Gaddi the while, whose eyes were starting from his head with terror, and who was more than half dead. "Agnolo," I said to him, "this is no time to shiver and shake. Up and make yourself useful! Throw assafoetida on the fire." '

Soon after this the spirits gradually vanished, the magician gathered up a great load of books he had brought with him, and they all stepped cautiously out of the circle, the boy clutching Benvenuto by the cloak in his fright. Two of the demons they had seen in the Colosseum ran in front of them, now on the ground, now on the roof-tops. And that night they all dreamed of devils.

In the letters on natural magic he addressed to Sir Walter Scott, Sir David Brewster suggests that the Sicilian priest and his assistant produced these apparitions by means of one or more concave mirrors and lenses. A fire was lighted and perfumes and incense were burnt in order to create a ground for the images, and the spectators were rigidly confined within the pale of the magic circle. The concave mirror and the objects presented to it were so placed that Cellini and his companions within the circle could see neither them nor the aerial images of the objects by the rays directly reflected from the mirror. It was not necessary for the magician to attend on the mirror. He could take his place in the circle with the others. The images of the devils were all distinctly formed in the air immediately above the fire, but none of them was visible to those inside the circle until the perfumes were thrown into the fire and the wreaths of smoke reflected the appearances to the eyes of the watchers. More and more spectral figures would be manifested as the smoke was diffused.

The assafoetida was probably intended to stupefy Cellini and his friends still more and perhaps to encourage them to add phantoms of their own imagining to the demons they actually saw. Agnolino Gaddi and the boy were both so overcome with dread that they did indeed fancy things they could not have seen, but the boy's description of the four armed giants of colossal size who made as if to break into the circle precisely records the effect that would have been produced by pushing the figures closer to the mirror and then magnifying their images, thus causing them to advance towards the circle. The priest had perhaps fitted a concave mirror into a box containing the figures of the spectres and either he or his assistant carried home the box with its lights, thus accounting for the devils that went leaping and skipping in front of the party.

Although Cellini says that he was frightened during this second visit to the Colosseum, his account is not that of a man who believes he has been in touch with supernatural powers. In order to reassure the terrified boy he tells him that what he saw was 'only smoke and shade', and this suggests that the sculptor may have suspected something of the nature of the deception. This conclusion is borne out by the fact that a day or two later the necromancer tried in vain to interest Cellini in a project to accompany him as his paid assistant to a particular spot in the mountains of Norcia, where he promised to show him manifestations of a much more surprising character. He may have intended to combine his conjuring with the natural effects of reflection from concave surfaces sometimes witnessed in mountainous places. The Reverend T. S. Hughes, travelling in Sicily in 1830, noted that 'at the extremity of the vast shadow which Etna projects across the island appeared a perfect and distinct image of the mountain itself, elevated above the horizon and diminished, as if viewed in a convex mirror'. Many travellers have described the eerie appearance of the Spectre of the Brocken, the reflected spectrum of the observer upon the highest point of the Harz Mountains; and no one who has read it will be likely to forget James Hogg's remarkable evocation in *The Confessions of a Justified Sinner* of the giant shadow projected on to the morning mist from Arthur's Seat.

It is clear that skill was needed to create illusions by means of concave mirrors alone and that only an unsophisticated audience could be completely hoodwinked. But with the invention of the magic lantern in the seventeenth century, magicians were supplied with a tool which immensely enhanced their powers of producing convincing phantasms.

The magic lantern was invented by Athanasius Kircher in about 1640 and he outlines its principles in his book *Ars Magna Lucis et Umbrae*, first published in 1645. Kircher was a scientist of considerable repute, but he was also a Jesuit priest and from the little that is known about him he seems to have had much in common with the magician-priests of earlier ages. He discloses the same talent for showmanship, the same power of exciting and terrifying his audiences, and it was he who applied the epithet 'magic' to his apparatus.

The spectators of Kircher's shows were not placed as they usually were in

18

Victorian times and always are today—on the same side of the screen as the lantern: his screen was between the viewers and the lantern and was made of transparent taffetas. His pictures were painted on long strips of glass, every part of which was made opaque except the figures. By the skilful manipulation of his lantern Kircher could make these figures appear at one moment as big as giants, the next as small as dwarfs; they would advance, retire, dissolve into seeming nothingness, and then return in utterly different forms. On one occasion Kircher made mysterious handwriting materialize on the wall of a room from which he and his instrument were excluded; and on another, by combining the effects of the magic lantern with those of the newly invented polished cylindrical mirror (which is capable of creating a normal image from a distorted picture), the Jesuit stunned his audience by favouring them with a vision of the Ascension. No wonder he was regarded as a sorcerer.

Father Kircher was the last recorded ordained priest openly to concern himself with optics, and with him the link between religion and the summoning of spectral figures by means of mirror and lantern is severed. The art of projecting images was henceforth classified as an entertainment. Yet the effect it produced was very often as shattering as if it had been the work of supernatural agencies. Harriet Martineau, writing about the magic-lantern shows which were given at Christmas and once or twice a year during her childhood in the opening decade of the last century, says:

'I used to see it cleaned by daylight and to handle all its parts, understanding its whole structure; yet such was my terror of the white circle on the wall, and of the moving slides, that to speak the truth, the first apparition always brought on bowel-complaint; and, at the age of thirteen, when I was pretending to take care of little children during the exhibition, I could never look at it without having the back of a chair to grasp, or hurting myself to carry off the intolerable sensation.'

The same writer also mentions a form of magic-lantern entertainment which was directly related to Kircher's demonstrations and to the performances of the Sicilian priest witnessed by Cellini: the so-called Phantasmagoria. 'I did not like the darkness to begin with,' writes Miss Martineau, 'and when Minerva appeared, in a red dress, at first extremely small and then approaching until her owl seemed coming directly upon me, it was so like my nightmare dreams that I shrieked aloud.'

The Phantasmagoria, which functioned by means of a screen set up after the manner of Kircher between lantern and audience, was named by M. Philipsthal in 1802 when he exhibited it with enormous success in London and Edinburgh. It was not an altogether new form of entertainment, but Philipsthal, a mysterious character reported to have dabbled in alchemy after having been trained as a doctor, was a better showman than his predecessors and rivals. A sternly critical viewer, the scientist Sir David Brewster, has left a description of Philipsthal's procedure.

'The small theatre of exhibition,' he writes, 'was lighted only by one hanging lamp, the flame of which was drawn up into an opaque chimney or shade when the performance began. In this semi-obscurity the curtain rose and displayed a cave with skeletons and other terrific figures in relief upon its walls. The flickering light was then drawn up beneath its shroud, and the spectators, left in total darkness, found themselves in the midst of thunder and lightning. A thin transparent screen had, unknown to the spectators, been let down after the disappearance of the light, and upon it the flashes of lightning and all the subsequent appearances were represented. The thunder and lightning were followed by the figures of ghosts, skeletons, and known individuals whose eyes and mouths were made to move by the shifting of combined slides. After the first figure had been exhibited for a short time, it began to grow less and less, as if removed to a great distance, and at last vanished in a small cloud of light. Out of this same cloud another figure began to appear and gradually grew larger and larger and approached the spectator until it attained its perfect development.'

One of Philipsthal's favourite tricks was to show the head of Dr. Franklin and to transform it slowly into a skull. He also presented fully dressed persons who retired from the spectators with all the freshness of life, only to come into view again a moment later in the form of grisly skeletons; these skeletons were then clothed step by step, first with flesh and then with appropriate garments. The performance generally ended with a mustering of ghosts, skeletons, and monsters, who with one accord advanced upon the trembling audience,

Optic toys in the Barnes Collection, including a rackwork slide, Thaumatrope discs, a Zoetrope, a Phenakistiscope, a Praxinoscope, peep-eggs, and a cylindrical mirror with polyoptic pictures, together with various magic lanterns, a Kinora, and a Projecting Phenakistiscope on the shelf behind

becoming larger and larger as they drew near, just as in Harriet Martineau's account, only to sink into the ground as they seemed about to seize the onlookers, many of whom avowed that the phantoms looked so solid they felt they could touch them.

Philipsthal's was the best-known but by no means the only phantasmagoria entertainment of the period. A Mr. Robertson, who had an establishment in Paris (in the Cour des Capucins on almost the same site where the first cinematograph theatre was to be opened more than a century later), varied his effects by introducing along with his pictures the direct, moving shadows of living persons, thus giving the impression of people going about on a dark night or in moonlight. According to the *Lady's Magazine* of 1802, some of the phantasmagoria shows seem to have appealed to very much the same kind of audience as the more exciting and spectacular of modern films. The proprietor of a phantasmagoria theatre in Dorset Mews put on a strip-tease act which would certainly have been marked 'X' today, although his audience was said to consist chiefly of 'young girls, boys, and women' (at half-a-crown-a-head admission). Parents complained at their children frequenting such a place and because the performance started so late that it was often after midnight when the girls and boys arrived home, and 'sometimes they did not come at all'. The showman and several of his assistants were apprehended and the magistrate took a serious view of the case, denouncing the Phantasmagoria as an evil and committing the proprietor to Bridewell.

A phantasmagoria lanternist at work. The glass slides were opaque except for the part forming the figures, and the images could be increased or diminished in size by moving the lantern farther away from or closer to the screen. The impression of movement might be still more enhanced by the shifting of combined slides. (Engraving after a painting by J. B. Schénau from Pugin's *Dictionnaire du Théâtre*)

2

Peepshows and Panoramas

To peep at such a world—to see the stir
Of the great Babel, and not feel the crowd.
COWPER

THE aerial images projected by magicians with the aid of concave mirrors, and the phantoms flung upon the screen by the lantern, were the distant ancestors of the fantastic, irrational, magical aspects of the film. The early peepshows and the panoramas and dioramas which developed from them provided a more prosaic element: they were the forerunners of modern travelogues and newsreels. With them, too, the moving picture was for the first time enclosed in a definite frame. And peepshows and panoramas were not projections of three-dimensional bodies, they were essentially two-dimensional images to which a third dimension was added by means of perspective, special lenses, and transmitted or reflected light.

Peepshows and panoramas have much in common with the camera obscura, substituting a painted and controlled image for the haphazard actual scene reflected in the darkened chamber. A primitive form of camera obscura was known as early as the fourth century B.C. in Greece. Leonardo experimented with it and noted that 'if the images of illuminated objects are reflected through a small aperture into a very dark room, they can be thrown on to a piece of white paper, their shapes and colour being perfectly preserved'. And in his *Magica Naturalis*, published in 1553, Giovanni della Porta gives a detailed description of the mechanism of the camera obscura.

A convex lens is fitted into the only opening through which light can

23

penetrate into a darkened chamber, and rays of light passing through it from any outside object form a reduced and inverted image which is received on a reflecting mirror inclined at an angle of 45 degrees and flung on to a sheet of paper or a plate of ground glass on a table inside the room. Go up into the little tower containing the camera obscura at Portmeirion, stare at the pale round table in the pitchy room, and you will see a miniature moving picture of all that you have left outside. Waiters are carrying out trays of tea to groups of people sitting on the grassy terrace by the estuary, an old gentleman blows his nose with a large blue handkerchief as he lowers himself into his deck-chair, a girl with two retrievers comes along the path towards you and runs right off the table.

The camera obscura overlooking the Avon gorge at Bristol is even more astonishing, for here a handle inside the darkened room enables you to turn the inclined mirror to reflect images from all quarters, and the pictures flung on to the white concave table measure 6 ft. across and are big enough to reveal subtle changes in expression during an observed conversation. You can watch it all without yourself being seen, and because the people and objects in the picture are so curiously diminished and so strangely lifted from their actual surroundings into the picture rectangle they take on a significance which they do not have when seen normally by the naked eye.

The camera obscura can show only the scenes and incidents in its immediate vicinity which are reflected into its lens; the peepshow makes use of mirrors and sometimes of lenses to yield glimpses of distant, long-vanished, or legendary scenes. It usually takes the form of a box with a small eye-piece through which we peep at the receding elements of a perspective view. Alberti is supposed to have made such a peepshow in about 1437 to illustrate the laws of perspective; it was illuminated from the back and changes in the lighting produced effects of daylight, moonlight, or storm. This peepshow was a scientific toy for educated adults and it was followed during the Renaissance period by others of a similar character, some of them very complicated and combined with clocks.

There are three exquisitely fashioned clock peepshows in the collection of the Kunsthistorisches Museum in Vienna made by the German clockmaker Marggraf, who is known to have based them on the camera obscura. In both subject-matter and the design of the framework these peepshows closely follow the pattern of the court theatre of the sixteenth century. Yet the relationship between theatre and peepshow is quite different from that between theatre and toy theatre. The latter is a miniature version of the original, whereas the peepshow substitutes a reflected picture for the direct image, suggesting the original by tricks of lighting and perspective.

The most intricate of Marggraf's creations consists of a rectangular box into the front of which a clock-face is built, while the left side is pierced by a glass-covered opening. The lid opens to an angle of 45 degrees and a mirror fixed inside it reflects an oval frame within the box. When this frame is lowered the viewer sees reflected in the mirror an enchanting grotto where Acteon has come upon Diana standing upon a pedestal. The scene is modelled in wax and set against a painted background. Seen in the mirror and cunningly lit, it ceases to be an artificial little group disposed in a box, and, like the pictures revealed by the camera obscura, it takes on a magical life of its own.

The second of Marggraf's peepshows is constructed without a hinged lid. You peep through a slit-like opening in the upper part of the box and become part of a ravishing scene, a brilliant reflection in an inclined mirror. A delight-fully rounded and feminine Athena lies stretched in sleep against a trophy of arms, her owl beside her, while behind her recumbent form ships are tossing on a choppy sea.

The third peepshow is imperfect, the tableau having vanished, but it provides a welcome opportunity for examining the structure of the box. It becomes apparent that the remarkable plastic effect of Marggraf's scenes was achieved not only by means of the inclined mirror above the subject but by additional mirrors in the side walls of the structure.

The makers of seventeenth-century peepshows preferred scenes from everyday life to those taken from the classical themes of contemporary drama. A lens was usually by this time fitted into the eye-piece, and this both enlarged the image and enhanced the three-dimensional effect, but, even so, the ingenuity with which these peepshows were designed leaves one open-mouthed. Flat pictures on the walls of a square box were transformed by sheer skill in perspective into three-dimensional receding views.

A peepshow of this kind, but triangular in shape, was exhibited in London in 1656. It showed the interior of the Great Church at Haarlem and may have been the work of Samuel van Hoogstraaten (1627–1678), the most talented of several Dutch makers of 'perspective boxes'. As a youth of nineteen, he was already so famous for the exceptional optical cunning of his paintings that he was invited to Vienna by the Emperor Ferdinand III, and it may well have been Marggraf's peepshows, then in the royal collection, which turned Hoogstraaten's attention to this fascinating form of illusion. From this time he was passionately interested in optics, and his friend, the art historian Arnold Houbraken, relates that his house was full of cut cardboard representations of fruit, fish, people, animals, and buildings, which appeared to have three dimensions.

Hoogstraaten's peepshow in the London National Gallery shows the interior of a Dutch house painted only on the sides and bottom of a box, yet creating the illusion of three-dimensional reality so perfectly that it is difficult to believe that this is not a very superior doll's house tenanted by miniature models of real persons. Tiles, two chairs, and a dog are painted partly on the bottom, partly on the sides, of the box, and a table is painted entirely on the floor. The tricks of perspective are supported in this case by several inclined mirrors.

At the beginning of the eighteenth century, peepshows were made in Holland which differed from those already described in that they consisted neither of a tableau arranged against a perspective background, nor of a perspective view painted on the sides and bottom of a box, but of several panels of glass set up one behind another, seen through a lens and lit from behind. Seventeenth-century peepshows such as those of Hoogstraaten had already diverged from the theatrical tradition in their choice of subject-matter and arrangement, and those of the eighteenth century differed still more, concentrating on the presentation of celebrated views and historical events.

Of those which were shown publicly, and which from engravings appear often to have been of considerable size, nearly all have vanished, but small versions of them survive in children's peepshows. In many of these the scenes are composed of wood, cardboard, or stiff paper instead of glass, and very often the opening at the back for light effects is filled with coloured oiled paper. Some of the most delightful of these were made at Augsburg at the beginning of the eighteenth century by the brothers Engelbrecht. They are engraved with all the traditional skill of this ancient centre of great engravers, and show perspectives of formal gardens with fountains and statues, baroque halls, and hilly landscapes.

Toy peepshows continued to be made throughout the nineteenth century. Favourite subjects included the *Opening of the Thames Tunnel* (a particularly good example of which, by Heinrich Keller, is in the R. J. Abbey collection), *The Great Exhibition of 1851*, and *The Coronation of Queen Victoria*—which had its modern counterpart in the publication in 1953 by Hulton Press of *The Coronation of Her Majesty Queen Elizabeth II*, in the form of a concertina-type folding peepshow made by Edwin Smith. Both these coronation peepshows allowed the viewer to peep through the rose window of the Abbey. In the Victorian example the ceremony can be seen taking place in the dim recesses of the great church, while the modern production shows the Queen sweeping up the main aisle with the peers and peeresses of the realm after the ceremony. The actual coronation can be witnessed through another peephole at the east end of the Abbey.

Some Victorian toy peepshows took the enchanting form of alabaster eggs, and were known as peep-eggs. Each egg contained two scenes viewed through a double convex lens mounted in the top of the body. Inside, three surfaces fixed in a metal spindle supported the scenes, which might be brought into view by turning two knobs which protruded from either side. The scenes were lit either by sunshine or artificial light shining through the translucent alabaster. A peep-egg in the collection of the Barnes brothers at Mousehole shows wonderfully plastic changing views of the Clifton Suspension Bridge and Nightingale Valley.

The large peepshows of which these toys were miniature versions were still being exhibited in the streets and on fairgrounds within living memory. The showmen carried their boxes on their backs and for a penny, or sometimes even for a halfpenny, spectators were allowed to peep at some sensational scene from contemporary life to the accompaniment of a commentary and occasionally of music played on a concertina.

A peepshow at a village fair is described by Dickens in *Our Mutual Friend*. It had originally started by being the Battle of Waterloo, but the showman had since made it into every other battle of subsequent date by altering the shape of the Duke of Wellington's nose. Other characteristic peepshow subjects included *The Mail Coach setting off from the Post Office*, *The Coronation of George IV*, *Queen Victoria's Visit to the City of London*, *Napoleon's Battle of the Pyramids*, and *The Mutiny on the Bounty*.

William Penkethman, the popular comedian and booth manager, was one of the many showmen to travel with peepshows during the eighteenth century, and another well-known exhibitor was Lord George Sanger's father. His peepshow was a large box fitted with six viewing holes, each provided with a strong lens. The spectators stood in front of the box, which had been set up on a folding trestle, and while they were peeping they were shut off from the crowds by a green curtain suspended round them on projecting rods. The scenes they saw were let down one after another on strings and were lit by a row of tallow candles. They consisted principally of various aspects of the Battle of Trafalgar, very brightly coloured, for James Sanger had fought on the *Victory* and could accompany his display with first-hand details of every sanguinary incident. He was so successful that he was able to buy a caravan and exhibit a peepshow which possessed twenty-six lenses, enabling twenty-six people to view it at the same time. The pictures were pulled up and down in rapid succession and their subjects were mainly melodramas, based on some recent tragedy fresh in the minds of the audience, like *The Murder in the Red Barn.*

The peepshow, which was known in the seventeenth century as a 'perspective box', was one of the fruits of the artist's passionate study of the laws of perspective. During the eighteenth century this enthusiasm for perspective was gradually yielding to a preoccupation with the effects of light. The trend was encouraged by the developing art of landscape and also by the fashionable use of the camera obscura in portable form as an aid to drawing the popular topographical views of the time. Sometimes lenses were even built into the tops of travelling coaches with their blinds drawn to transform them into dark rooms. By means of a mirror placed at an angle to reflect the incoming light, a picture of the scene outside was projected on to a board so that the artist could study it without exposing himself to the elements.

It was the fascination of transforming light shining or suddenly obscured behind translucent pictures painted on glass that led to the metamorphosis of the peepshow into the great popular entertainments, the Panorama and the Diorama. The painter Philip de Loutherbourg, experimenting with receding scenes lit from behind, hit on the brilliant idea of turning the peepshow into a

Japanese magic mirror, about 14 in. long, made of metal with a perfectly plain, highly polished, slightly convex face. When the rays of the sun are reflected from it the image of the leaves and berries on the back is distinctly seen upon the wall. (Barnes Collection)

The cylindrical mirror became a popular toy during the nineteenth century, though it was invented long before that. The polished metal cylinder reflected coherent images from distorted drawings called polyoptic pictures. Those shown here are coloured lithographs by Walter Fres. (Barnes Collection)

picture house which, like the camera obscura, would hold the spectators as well as the moving image and would exhibit scenes marvellously animated by means of light and so cunningly depicted that they could be viewed directly with as great an illusion of plasticity as if seen through a lens.

Like Hoogstraaten, Philip Jacob de Loutherbourg was a restless character, as much interested in mechanics and optics as in painting. He was born in Strasbourg in 1740 and came to England with an introduction to Garrick in 1771, having already made a name as a landscape painter in Paris, where he had been elected a member of the French Academy. Garrick engaged him to paint scenes for Drury Lane, a post for which his talents perfectly fitted him. He not only designed for the theatre but made important contributions to the improvement of stage mechanics. He was particularly clever at suggesting fog, fire, moonlight, and volcanic eruptions, and was the first artist in western Europe to devise an act drop or scenic curtain. It showed a romantic landscape based on a scene in Derbyshire and was first used in 1774 for a pantomime. Loutherbourg exhibited each year at the Academy and in 1781 was elected R.A. In the year of his election, curiously enough, however, he submitted no picture to Somerset House. The omission was noted by Walpole who wrote: 'Loutherbourg, being employed on his Eidophusikon, had no pictures for the Exhibition.'

The painter had been working on his invention for about twenty years, and in February 1781 he left the theatre and opened his romantically named Eidophusikon in a room in his house in Lisle Street. Contemporary accounts give no precise description of the mechanism of the Eidophusikon. W. D. Parke in his *Musical Memoirs*, published in 1830, speaks of Loutherbourg's 'newly invented transparent shades upon which was shed a vast body and brilliancy of colour producing an almost enchanting effect'. The pictures themselves were probably painted on very fine material in translucent colours, and light was then projected on to them from behind at variable distances through adjustable coloured glass, added lustre being obtained by means of reflecting mirrors. The scenes were shown through an aperture measuring 8 by 6 ft.

The performance on the opening day, February 26th, 1781, started with a vision of dawn over London seen from Greenwich Hill. The distant city lay

Above: Peepshow at Bartholomew Fair. The showman would pull the pictures up and down by means of strings, disclosing one scene after another illumined by a row of tallow candles. He would accompany the show with a commentary and sometimes with concertina music. Fairground peepshows might be fitted with up to twenty-six eyepieces, usually supplied with lenses

Below: View through the peephole of Samuel van Hoogstraaten's seventeenth-century 'perspective box'. The scene is painted on the walls of the box, the stereoscopic effect being achieved by tricks of perspective aided by inclined mirrors. (National Gallery, London)

shrouded in mist, which gradually lifted as the sun grew stronger. Cattle loomed up in the foreground grazing in Greenwich Park, while as the day advanced more and more shipping moved up and down the Thames. This scene was followed by a musical interval, the music being specially chosen to harmonize with the picture. Then came a dramatic rendering of a storm at sea, accompanied by wild music, and next, in quick succession, seasonal scenes of rural life, a stupendous sunset, a fight between peasants and wolves in the Swiss Alps, and finally the English Fleet advancing to the relief of Gibraltar.

The spectators' receptivity was greatly encouraged by the darkened auditorium, an aid to illusion and a feature of all the successors of the Eidophusikon which was not found in the theatre at that time. It was not until the late nineteenth century that Irving introduced the practice of lighting only the stage during a performance. He also used transparent lacquers for the glasses of his limes to get subtle tones and suggest moonlight and sunset effects, prompted to these innovations by his study of the work of Loutherbourg.

In 1782 Loutherbourg added a new series to his moving pictures, the themes including *The Cataract of Niagara* and *Satan arraying his Troops on the Bank of the Fiery Lake, with the Raising of the Palace of Pandemonium; from Milton*. This last was supported by more than music: the delighted audience was almost deafened by the dreadful sounds appropriate to this horrific scene. As legions of hideous shrieking demons arose at the summons of their chief, a volcano began to erupt liquid fire to the accompaniment of lightning and claps of thunder. 'The lightning,' wrote a viewer, 'exhibits all the vivid and varied flashes of that natural phenomenon and the thunder includes every vibration of air and shock of element which so often in its prototype strike terror and admirations on the mind.'

Gainsborough, who repeatedly visited the Eidophusikon and often helped Loutherbourg to manipulate the scenes, was once present at the showing of *Satan arraying his Troops* when the fake storm was challenged by real thunder going on outside. Some of the spectators were terrified, believing this to be a warning sent by God against presumption, but Loutherbourg was transported with pleasure. 'By God, Gainsborough,' he cried, seizing the painter by the arm, 'our thunder's best!' As a direct result of his admiration of the Eidophusikon, Gainsborough constructed a peepshow for himself with twelve scenes painted on glass to be illuminated from the back. They are on view, lit up, in the Victoria and Albert Museum, and show cows at a watering-place, distant hills, woody landscapes, and ships in an estuary.

Loutherbourg eventually sold his Eidophusikon to a Mr. Chapman, who had been associated with its management, and it moved from the West End to the City and then went on long years of provincial tour. Its creator moved to Hammersmith Terrace and it soon became the talk of the town that he was devoting himself to miracle-working. At one time such enormous crowds flocked to seek his aid that the traffic at Hammersmith was completely disorganized and the streets full of rioters. This strange enthusiasm of his later years, so unexpected in a gifted painter and inventor, links Loutherbourg with Kircher and the Sicilian priest, who also combined the exercise of faith with the practice of optical conjuring.

The Eidophusikon was destroyed by fire at the beginning of the last century, but not before it had inspired the invention of the Panorama and all the other 'oramas' which played so prominent a part in the social life of the Regency and Victorian periods. It is seldom now remembered that there were almost as many houses showing entertainments of this kind in the London of a hundred and twenty years ago as there are cinemas today. There were establishments in Leicester Square, the Strand, Regent's Park, Regent Street, Oxford Street, St. James's Street, King Street, Hyde Park Corner, Waterloo Place, the Haymarket, Piccadilly, and Adelaide Street; and both the Theatre Royal, Covent Garden, and Drury Lane enlivened their repertoire by the inclusion of dioramas. Just as the programmes of the early cinema theatres would be punctuated by an interval performance by a stage artiste, a popular musician or comedian, so the play at Covent Garden would be interrupted by such forerunners of the film as the *Moving Diorama of the Polar Expedition, being a series of views representing the progress of His Majesty's ships the* Hecla *and* Envy *in their endeavours to discover a North-West Passage from the Atlantic to the Pacific Ocean* (one of David Robert's productions), while the audience at Drury Lane would be regaled with Clarkson Stanfield's *Grand Moving Picture of a Voyage to the Isle of Wight including a visit to Cowes Regatta.*

The craze for these early news and travel movies spread all over Europe and to the principal American towns, and gave rise to a crop of inventions of similar forms of entertainment, among them being the Betaniorama, the Cyclorama, the Europerama, the Cosmorama, the Giorama, the Pleorama,

the Kalorama, the Kineorama, the Poecilorama, the Neorama, the Nausorama, the Octorama, the Physiorama, the Typorama, the Udorama, and the
Uranorama.

The popularity of these entertainments was even reflected in the fashionable
slang of the time. 'The recent invention of the Diorama,' writes Balzac in
Le Père Goriot, 'which had carried optical illusion one stage farther than the
Panorama, had led in some studios to the pleasantry of talking "rama", and a
young painter who frequented the Maison Vauquer had inoculated the boarders
with the disease. "Well, Monsieur-r-r Poiret," said the museum official, "how
is your little healthorama?" ' And a minute or two later Vautrin says, 'It's
desperately chillyorama', and as the soup is served Poiret cries out, 'Ah! here
comes a fine souporama', and the company is soon talking about a goriorama
and a cornorama.

The invention of the Panorama is usually attributed to Robert Barker, an
Edinburgh painter. In about 1785 he was put into prison for debt and was
confined to a cell lit by a grating let into the wall at the junction of wall and
ceiling. One day he was reading a letter and to see more clearly carried it below
the grating. The effect when the paper was held in the shaft of light falling from
the opening was so astonishing that Barker's imagination was set working on
the possibilities of controlled light flung from above upon pictures of large
dimensions. He had already seen the amazing results achieved by Loutherbourg
with lights behind the picture. He now conceived of something much more
ambitious.

Barker's new picture entertainment was patented on June 19th, 1787, the
patent referring, however, not to the 'Panorama', a word which had not yet
been coined, but to 'an entire new contrivance or apparatus called by him
"*La nature à coup d'œil*" '. Later in the same year the artist exhibited a large
semi-circular view of Edinburgh in that city. The huge concave picture, which
the audience could glimpse out of the corners of their eyes as well as straight in
front of them, must have had something of the effect of the modern cinerama.

But this was only a stage in the development of the Panorama proper,
which Barker first showed at his premises in Leicester Square in 1792. It was a
view of the English Fleet at anchor between Portsmouth and the Isle of Wight,
and consisted of an enormous canvas attached to the inside of a rotunda 16 ft.
high and 45 ft. in diameter, which revolved slowly round the spectators seated

in the centre. An engraving of the machinery of a panorama reproduced in the *Journal de Genie Civil* in 1800 shows that it much resembled the structure of a post mill. Placed in semi-darkness in the middle of a circle which recalled the magic circles formerly described by sorcerers and conjurers of spirits, the audience gazed across a gulf of as much as 12 ft. at a continuous, moving view of an entire region, drawn with such ingenious perspective and so skilfully lit from above that, according to contemporary reviewers, the illusion was perfect.

Barker's assistant at these performances was Robert Fulton, an American, later to become famous for his invention of the steamship. He had started life as a blacksmith and afterwards studied painting under Benjamin West. Barker and Fulton together followed up the panorama of the English Fleet, which had met with a wildly enthusiastic reception, with a *View of London*, *Lord Howe's Naval Victory over the French*, *The Battle of Aboukir*, *Brighthelmstone*, and *The Environs of Windsor*. Fulton then went over to Paris with Barker's invention, while Barker himself took his panorama first on a tour of the English provinces and then to Germany, where he gave it the unattractive name of the Nausorama. *The English Fleet* was accorded a rapturous welcome at Hamburg in 1799, while Leipzig audiences queued for hours to see the *View of London* and *Lord Howe's Naval Victory*.

A visit to Barker's panorama prompted a painter from Magdeburg, Breysig, to set up a panorama of his own. He built a rotunda in Berlin and collaborated with another painter called Kaaz in the production in 1800 of a *View of Rome*, a characteristically German choice of subject. The performance was very highly praised by the Press, Kaaz being specially acclaimed for his rendering of the figures and vegetation. The Berlin panorama later became well known for its up-to-date news items: in 1812 it showed the burning of Moscow only three months after the actual event had taken place.

Panoramas now began to multiply in all the capitals of Europe. A notable *View of Vienna*, painted from drawings made by William Barton, was exhibited at the panorama established in Vienna by Professor Jansche and the painter Postle; and Van de Watt's institution in Amsterdam, known as La Gueldre, was famous.

Meanwhile, in Paris, Fulton, who was anxious to give up painting altogether so that he could devote himself to his steam-boat project, sold the patent he had taken out on his arrival in France to an American couple, Mr. and

C   33

Mrs. James Thayer. They immediately built two rotundas, each 17 metres in diameter, on the boulevard Montmartre. The site of these structures, which have long since vanished, is commemorated in the name of an alley, the Passage des Panoramas. From 1800 onwards the Thayers put on a continuous show daily from 8 a.m. till 8 p.m., the entrance price being 1 fr. 50 for each adult. One of the rotundas showed a *View of Paris* painted by Jaan Mouchet, Pierre Prévost, and Constant Bourgeois, while the other exhibited *The Evacuation of Toulon by the English in 1793*, painted by Pierre Prévost and Constant Bourgeois. Prévost soon became the most outstanding panorama artist in Paris; so popular, indeed, that his name is often mistakenly associated with the actual invention of this form of moving picture. Two of the most successful of his early panoramas were said to have been *Napoleon's Camp at Boulogne* and a *View of Amsterdam*.

The French regarded these panoramas not merely as entertainment but as serious educational exhibitions; they ascribed to them a value similar to that attributed to documentary films today. A special committee of the Institut de France was formed in 1800 to report on the invention and its conclusions were that the Panorama 'merited the interest and approbation of the Institute which ought to testify its satisfaction to citizen James Thayer and the artists and urge them to redouble their efforts to achieve new successes which would earn them the ever-increasing approval of the educated public and the benevolence of the Government'.

An English viewer of much the same standing as the members of the French Institute, Sir George Beaumont, expressed another point of view, condemning the Panorama rather as some connoisseurs of art of our own time are inclined to disparage the cinema, as injurious to the taste of both artists and the public.

At least one practising French painter is known to have been wholly in favour of the new invention. David was so overwhelmed by the spectacle and by Prévost's skill that he turned to the pupils he had brought with him crying, '*Vraiment, Messieurs, c'est ici qu'il faut venir pour étudier la nature!*' It is indeed easier to imagine this stiff neo-Classic studying nature in the rotundas on the boulevard Montmartre than in the open fields, and more weight should be attached to the opinion of a man who worked all his life from nature and revolutionized the art of landscape. Constable, who went in 1803 to see a view of Rome executed by Reinagle and Barker, said that the style exactly suited the whole conception and that great principles should neither be expected nor looked for in such a medium of expression. He enjoyed the Panorama for its ingenuity and as a charming distraction.

In 1807 Thayer and Prévost joined forces and opened a new rotunda between the rue Neuve-Saint-Augustin and the boulevard des Capucines. It measured 31 metres across and exhibited pictures of the enormous dimensions of 110 by 16 metres. The central circular platform for the spectators held a hundred and fifty people and was about 12 metres from the screen. Prevost's favourite subjects all glorified the career of the Emperor and included *The Battle of Wagram* and *The Meeting at Tilsit between Napoleon and Alexander I.* The artist intended to immortalize eight of Napoleon's victories and his efforts had already won the Emperor's approval when they were cut short by the events of 1812. In 1816 Prévost travelled to the Near East to make detailed studies for projected panoramas of Jerusalem, Athens, and Constantinople. He completed the first two, but died in 1823 before he could start work on the painting of Constantinople.

In England Prévost's heroic themes and vast proportions were paralleled by the spectacles offered by Charles Marshall at Spring Gardens. He showed the Battles of Ligny, les Quatres Bras, and Waterloo painted on 10,000 sq. ft. of canvas and constituting what he called his 'Peristrophic Panoramas'.

Panoramas were still being exhibited in Barker's original rotunda in Leicester Square, which was later taken over by Robert Burford and moved to the Strand, where Burford collaborated with Barker's son, Henry Aston Barker. At the Coliseum, a building erected in Regent's Park from designs by Decimus Burton, panoramas of London, Paris, and Lisbon enjoyed a great vogue. The establishment was run by a showman inventor and painter called William George Horner, who introduced some novel ideas. The *View of London* he exhibited in 1829 was seen from the top of St. Paul's and based on sketches Horner had made while repairs were being done and the dome surrounded by scaffolding. He so contrived the show that the audience, after passing through a dark, narrow corridor, entered a lift and were taken up in total obscurity to what appeared to be the dome of the Cathedral, and then entered a lantern from which they saw the City bathed in light stretching out beneath them. This ambitious spectacle met with a favourable reception, but it could never become a staple item in the repertoire of the Coliseum because the lighting effects were so difficult to manage. On sunny days an unwanted shadow would be cast across the painting by the audience suspended above the scene, and the illusion would be sadly impaired. A French writer remarked that it was only in London, where the public had no aesthetic sensibility, that so crude a performance would be tolerated. Be that as it may, the straightforward panoramas of Rome and Paris brought in better returns than the *View of London* and continued to be shown until the Coliseum was destroyed in 1875.

Meanwhile a new entertainment, or rather another and grander version of the Eidophusikon, had been introduced to the public by Jacques Mande Daguerre, better known as the author of the daguerreotype, and Charles Marie Bouton. Both these men had worked as assistants to Prevost, Bouton as a painter and Daguerre as an expert in lighting and scenic effects. Their invention consisted of gigantic transparent pictures exhibited under changing light. The screens, of which there were usually two adjoining each other at an angle, remained stationary, while the auditorium, a cylindrical room with a single opening in the wall like the proscenium of a theatre, slowly turned, moving the spectators from one part of the picture to another and from one picture to another and giving the impression that the image was animated. The first Diorama, a plain building with long windows, was designed by Daguerre himself and erected in the rue Sanson in the heart of Paris. On the opening day, July 11th, 1822, two dioramas were exhibited: *The Valley of the Sarnen in Canton Unterwalden, Switzerland*, by Daguerre and *The Interior of Trinity Chapel, Canterbury Cathedral*, by Bouton. The following description of the performance written by an English spectator, Frederick Bakewell, vividly recaptures the experience of an afternoon at the rue Sanson:

'The visitors, after passing through a gloomy anteroom, were ushered into a circular chamber, apparently quite dark. One or two small shrouded lamps placed on the floor served dimly to light the way to a few descending steps and the voice of an invisible guide gave directions to walk forward. The eye soon became sufficiently accustomed to the darkness to distinguish the objects around and to perceive that there were several persons seated on benches opposite an open space resembling a large window. Through the window was seen the interior of Canterbury Cathedral undergoing partial repair with the figures of

Above: View through the centre eyepiece of a nineteenth-century French concertina-folding peepshow of the Place Vendôme
Below: View of the side of the same peepshow. It is lit from the sides instead of from the top as is often the case with concertina-folding peepshows

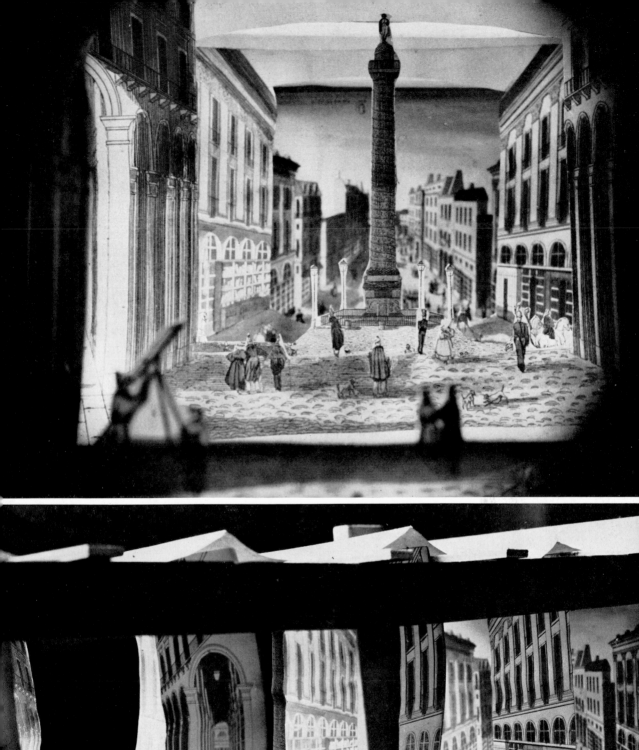

Engraving from a review of Daguerre's diorama *Ruins in a Fog* shown at the Regent's Park Diorama in June 1827

Painting by Daguerre, based on his diorama of Holyrood Chapel, shown at the Regent's Park Diorama in 1826. (Walker Art Gallery, Liverpool)

two or three workmen resting from their labours. The pillars, the arches, the stone floor and steps, stained with damp, and the planks of wood strewn on the ground, all seemed to stand out in bold relief, so solidly as not to admit a doubt of their substantiality, whilst the floor extended to the distant pillars, temptingly inviting the tread of exploring footsteps. Few could be persuaded that what they saw was a mere painting on a flat surface. The impression was strengthened by perceiving the light and shadows change, as if clouds were passing over the sun, the rays of which occasionally shone through the painted windows, casting coloured shadows on the floor. Then shortly the lightness would disappear and the former gloom again obscure the objects that had been momentarily illumined. The illusion was rendered more perfect by the sensitive condition of the eye in the darkness of the surrounding chamber.

'While gazing in wrapt admiration at the architectural beauties of the cathedral the spectator's attention was disturbed by sounds underground. He became conscious that the scene before him was slowly moving away and he obtained a glimpse of another and very different prospect, which gradually advanced until it was completely developed and the cathedral had disappeared. What he now saw was a valley surrounded by high mountains capped with snow.'

The Diorama enjoyed from the first a brilliant, a sensational, success and soon surpassed the Panorama as a form of popular entertainment. *The Times* reporter referred scornfully to panorama paintings as 'coarse sketches' in comparison with the Diorama. More than one reviewer refused to believe that the water in Daguerre's *Valley of the Sarnen* was only painted, another extolled this scene as more beautiful than nature, while a writer in the *Journal de Paris* stated that the invention constituted an epoch in the history of painting and could not fail to enlarge the boundaries of art by showing painters how to combine new effects.

It is illuminating to compare this naive eulogy, based on the credo that art is and cannot be other than the exact reproduction of nature, with the opinion of a true artist. Constable, who, it will be remembered, had visited the Panorama during his early years in London, was invited to a private view of the two diorama scenes just described in 1823 when Daguerre, encouraged by his phenomenal success in Paris, had set up a second establishment in London. 'It is in part a transparency', says Constable in a letter to his friend Archdeacon Fisher; 'the spectator is in a dark chamber, and it is very pleasing and has great illusion. It is without the pale of the art, because its object is deception. The art pleases by *reminding* not by *deceiving*. The place was filled with foreigners, and I seemed to be in a cage of magpies.'

The two subjects of the first Diorama each measured 71½ by 45½ ft. They were lit both from above and from behind, and the remarkable diverse effects were produced by combinations of transparent and opaque painting and by light transmitted through ground glass and coloured translucent screens on to the front of the picture, and through it from the back by means of long, vertical ground-glass windows, which could be shuttered when necessary or covered partially or entirely with pieces of coloured glass worked by pulleys and counterweights. The complicated machinery by means of which the audience was revolved was so cleverly contrived that it could be worked by a single man, who turned a crank at the signal of a bell. At the back of the rotunda there were nine boxes which seated forty people, while three hundred and ten more were accommodated in the amphitheatre. As in the Panorama, the spectators were divided by about 40 ft. from the picture, and screens stretching from the proscenium to the picture edges formed a broad tunnel which concentrated the gaze and gave added depth to the image. Performances were continuous from 11 a.m. till 4 p.m. and the price of admission was 3 francs for the boxes and 2 francs for the amphitheatre, nearly twice the cost of a visit to the Panorama.

Until 1831 there were always two diorama pictures on view at the rue Sanson, and after that date there were three. One of Daguerre's most spectacular dioramas was the *Midnight Mass at Saint-Etienne du Mont*, in which the church was first seen in the full light of day, empty, and then at midnight, illumined by candles and full of kneeling figures. It was shown together with a remarkable open-air transformation scene in which the disasters of a terrible landslide which took place at Goldau in Switzerland in 1806 were re-enacted.

Daguerre's London Diorama was built in Park Square East, Regent's Park. Nash designed the façade to form the centre part of the terrace on which he was working at the time; the rotunda was constructed by the elder Pugin, assisted by James Morgan, a civil engineer; and the actual machinery was the work of an engineer named Topham. It is one of the very few diorama buildings which still exists, for those that were not destroyed to make way for new developments almost inevitably fell prey to fire. The façade of the Regent's Park structure, with its three doors, remains unaltered except that the word 'DIORAMA', which once ran along the raised top, has been painted out. It opened to the public on September 29th, 1823, a ticket of admission costing 2s. The performances went on from 11 a.m. till 4, 5, or 6 p.m., according to the season; and during the darker months of winter the establishment was closed. Bouton was in charge of the London Diorama while Daguerre returned to Paris.

Until 1830 all the pictures shown in London were ones which had already appeared in Paris, and after they had been exhibited at Park Square East they were sent on to other dioramas which had been built in Liverpool, Dublin, and New York. The subjects shown were nearly all topographical; they included *The Ruins of Holyrood Chapel by Moonlight, Rosslyn Chapel, Effect of Sun, Effect of Fog and Snow seen through a Ruined Colonnade, The Port of Brest, The Village of Unterseen*, and *View of Paris from Montmartre*, all by Daguerre; and *The City of Rouen, St. Cloud, The Campo Vaccino, Rome, The Basilica of St. Paul without the Walls, Rome, The Ruins of Fountains Abbey*, and *The Interior of the Church of Santa Croce, Florence*, by Bouton.

Bouton's pieces were on the whole more factual and severely architectural than those of Daguerre, and his only attempt at creating an atmosphere of mystery and poetry, the *Santa Croce*, was a close imitation of Daguerre's *Midnight Mass*, except that Bouton enhanced the effect by installing a Grand Machine Organ which played the *Kyrie* from Haydn's Mass No. 1 during the midnight service. Bouton's *Coronation of Queen Victoria* was more in the nature of a newsreel and the fact that it did not appear until some two years after the celebration did not in the least detract from its success.

The Shrine of the Nativity, Bethlehem, though treated in a purely factual way, struck a different note and became one of the more popular and most frequently shown of the dioramas. It was designed by Charles Caius Renoux, who ran the Regent's Park establishment after Bouton returned to Paris in 1840. He was also the author of several double-effect pieces, among them *The Cathedral of Notre-Dame, Paris, The Interior of the Abbey Church of St. Ouen, Rouen*, and *View of Heidelberg*.

39

Renoux died in 1846 and when the Diorama opened for the 1847 season the public was offered the work of a new artist, Diosse, a pupil of Daguerre. His *Interior of St. Mark's, Venice*, was based on Bouton's *Santa Croce*. A daylight scene dissolved into a midnight service with kneeling figures to the accompaniment of the *Kyrie* from Mozart's Mass No. 12 instead of from the Haydn Mass chosen by Bouton. But Diosse followed this with a more original piece, a view of Mount Etna seen in three instead of two effects of light. The volcano was first glimpsed by moonlight, the romantic ruins of the theatre of Taormina dimly visible in the foreground. As day broke the whole noble landscape, the remains of antiquity and the snow-capped mountain sloping down to the vivid Ionian Sea came into view. The light increased until the scene sweltered under the full blaze of noon. Ominous rumbling was heard, flames began to mingle with the smoke rising from the crater, which a few moments later was belching red-hot lava to the crash of thunder and flash of lightning. Dense clouds of smoke and steam hung over the volcano, the sky was completely obscured, and it was only by the lurid glare from the molten fire rushing down the mountain-side that the audience could perceive the terrifying extent of the devastation wrought by the eruption.

Mount Etna was one of the two last dioramas to be shown at Regent's Park. The building became a Baptist chapel in 1855 and traces of this metamorphosis can still be seen in the Gothic buttresses supporting the masonry which partially fills the long windows of the former Diorama.

Back in Paris, Daguerre produced a fantastic *Beginning of the Deluge*, more robustly imaginative than any of his topographical pieces and distinctly reminiscent of Loutherbourg's *Satan arraying His Troops*. It is interesting to note that although this diorama was not shown to London audiences, Daguerre is listed in a dictionary compiled by Algernon Graves in 1884, of artists 'who have exhibited in the principle London Exhibitions of Oil Paintings from 1760–1880', as specializing in deluges, so it seems probable that he showed pictures in London which were either studies for the Diorama or pictorial versions done later.

Daguerre's Paris audiences were also treated to a thrilling murder story. They were transported to a solitary glade in the Black Forest, where the moon shone upon the blood-stained corpses of the Countess of Harzfeld and her servant. The murderers had only just left their victims and the fire they had kindled was still burning. The scene was so contrived that the spectators were made to feel as if the assassins were lurking in their immediate vicinity and might spring upon them at any moment. One reviewer was so overcome that he saw the performance three times in one week and in the end feared that only the poetry of Byron was adequate to express the intensity of his emotion.

A masterpiece of *trompe l'œil* by Daguerre in the church of Brie-sur-Marne, where this remarkable man passed the last ten years of his life, bears witness to his uncanny technical skill. The canvas, which shows a cathedral interior, hangs above the main altar and is so cunningly painted that the congregation seem to see a vast chancel, many times the size of the little church, stretching away into the dim recesses behind the altar.

An engraving of the diorama painting *Ruins in a Fog*, which appears in *The Mirror* of June 30th, 1827, and a picture by Daguerre in the Walker Art Gallery, Liverpool, of Holyrood Chapel by moonlight, first identified by Helmut Gernsheim in 1951, provide additional proof of the artist's perfect command of perspective drawing. The Liverpool picture, Mr. Gernsheim points out, was not a study for the Diorama of the same subject, but was done after the show had proved popular in the belief that a ready purchaser would be found for a 'still' of the moving picture. Daguerre used a camera obscura to make some of his preliminary sketches, and this may in part account for their photographic accuracy. Both the engraving of *Ruins in a Fog* and the picture of Holyrood, however, look as curiously stiff and lifeless as film photographs are apt to do. To catch something of the magic felt by Daguerre's audiences it is necessary to imagine all the paraphernalia that went with the show—the eerie approach through a dark passage, the dimly lit, circular auditorium and the bright screen on which effects came and went as the invisible showman and his assistants adjusted their lights and coloured glass. The text accompanying the engraving of *Ruins in a Fog* preserves much of the impression made by the spectacle:

'The subject of the above engraving is a novel illustration for our pages; as the fine old ruin is merely an imaginative design, and does not represent a real object: nevertheless, we are assured our engraving will have many admirers, as it is a faithful copy of one of the magnificent views now exhibiting at *The Diorama*.

'This fine picture represents a Gothic Gallery falling to decay, situate at the extremity of a narrow valley, beneath barren mountains. All is sombre, desolate and mournful; the long-drawn aisles, at a first glance, are alone perceived, for a thick fog reigns without, and such is the illusion of the scene, that you actually fancy yourself chilled by the cold and damp air. By degrees, however, the fog disperses and through the vast arches are plainly discovered the forests of pine and larch trees that cover the valley. The magic of this effect of light is indeed most extraordinary, and the illusion is complete and enchanting. The execution of this picture reflects the highest honour on Mr. Daguerres, the artist, whose talents have been frequently exercised on other subjects which have been exhibited at *The Diorama*, but with none of which we have been more interested, than the present specimen, which entitles Mr. Daguerres to be ranked as one of the most distinguished painters that ever lived.'

Spurred on by praise of this kind, Daguerre strove after ever greater fidelity to nature. He executed a *View of Mont Blanc* complete with a real chalet, barn, outhouses, and live goat eating hay which he had imported specially from Switzerland. But it was not a success; the actual objects killed rather than nourished the illusion.

The idea of combining an actual three-dimensional object with the diorama painting provided the inspiration of two other notable artists in this medium: Carl Wilhelm Gropius and Colonel Langlois. Gropius, who, like Loutherbourg, had been a scene painter, opened a diorama in Berlin in 1827, the building having been designed by his friend Carl Friedrich Schinkel. Gropius's pictures were rather smaller than those shown in Paris and London (65 by 42 ft.), but he introduced an improved lighting system by fitting long mirrors at an angle to the windows to cast reflected light on to the image. His subjects, like those of the other dioramas, were chiefly topographical and included a view of a rocky gorge near Sorrento, *The Grindelwald Glacier*, *The Harbour at Genoa from the Palazzo Doria*, and *The Scaliger Tombs at Verona*. One of his most striking exhibitions was of a Gothic cathedral at sunrise. The sun rose slowly to reveal an exquisite summer morning; boats on a canal gradually began to show signs of life; the great cathedral clock struck six; a hymn pealed forth on the organ through the open doors of the church, and people could be seen kneeling in prayer before a statue of the Virgin.

It was in 1832 that Gropius introduced his attempts at still-further-heightened realism, calling the show the Pleorama to distinguish it from the Diorama. He had taken the theme from the architect Langhaus of Breslau. The auditorium was constructed to resemble a small ship holding about thirty people, which sailed across the Bay of Naples or down the Rhine from Mainz to St. Goar, the movement of the picture and auditorium conspiring to give the impression of a changing viewpoint. This novel entertainment was, however, no more successful than Daguerre's Swiss chalet, though the fact that only thirty, instead of the usual two hundred or so, spectators could be admitted to the exhibition at a time may have made it uneconomical. Gropius, in any case, abandoned the Pleorama and went on showing his dioramas until 1850.

But the problem of combining natural objects and painting in the Diorama had already been solved as early as 1830 by Jean Charles Langlois. A fanatical soldier, born in 1789, he served both at Wagram and Waterloo, where he was conspicuous for his courage and was severely wounded. At the early age of twenty-six he was already a colonel and pensioned off. He resolved to devote his remaining years to the recording of the battles which for him represented the most intense experience that life could offer. Langlois had a certain facility for drawing, and he spent the first three years of his retirement studying under Girodet, depriving himself of all but the barest necessities in order to perfect himself in his art. He was interested only in military subjects, and the first canvas he was able to complete to his own satisfaction was hung in the Salon. Shortly after this, Langlois saw Prevost's Napoleonic panoramas and instantly realized that the Panorama was the ideal medium for reviving the scenes which were his passion. He gave up easel-painting for good, acquired a plot of ground in the rue de Marais du Temple, and built a rotunda to show pictures measuring 116 ft. 4 in. by 40 ft.

He called his shows, now panoramas, now dioramas, but they appear to have combined characteristics of both with effects derived from the Phantasmagoria. Instead of placing his audience at a distance from the scene of action, he transported them to the very centre of the battle by merging the three-dimensional auditorium so skilfully into the painted screen that it was impossible to tell where one ended and the other began.

Langlois's first subject, which was exhibited in 1830, was *The Battle of*

Navarin. An actual ship which had played a brilliant part in the engagement, the *Scipion*, was being broken up at the time and Langlois managed to get possession of the deck. He turned it into his auditorium, fusing it with the panorama picture by continuing the lines of the deck by means of illusionist painting across the gap which had previously divided the spectators from the screen. Below the deck Langlois constructed precise replicas of the captain's cabin, the officers' room, and the mess-room. The audience had to pass through rooms and along a narrow passage in a very dim light and then climb steep wooden steps through a hatchway. Once on deck they found themselves in the full light of midday and in the thick of the combat. A Turkish man-o'-war to the right of the *Scipion* had been struck, water was pouring into her gaping sides, the shrieks of the frantic crew could be heard, and several men were already struggling in the waves. A French frigate, the *Armide*, was in pursuit of an English vessel almost under the bows of the *Scipion*; another man-o'-war had burst into flames; the air was charged with the acrid smell of gunpowder, smoke veiled the distance and stung the eyes, and all the timbers of the *Scipion* shook at the repeated thunder of cannon.

That same year Langlois volunteered for the expedition to Algiers, and in 1835 he exhibited his second moving picture, *La Prise d'Alger*. His success enabled him to move to a rotunda in the Champs-Élysées with a larger proscenium, which had just been built. The first subject he showed there was *The Burning of Moscow*. Like Horner in his panorama of the city of London from St. Paul's, Langlois wanted his audience to look down on the scene. He placed them on one of the towers of the Kremlin and from this point of vantage they watched the fire spread rapidly to all parts of Moscow, drawing back terrified when it seemed as if the gigantic, crackling tongues of flame would mount to where they sat. And as they gazed they suddenly saw the Emperor and his guard fleeing from the conflagration. They passed along a narrow alley close to the palace and vanished from sight. Viewed as it was in smoke and flickering flamelight, Langlois's subject was probably more easily managed than Horner's broad-daylight panorama of London. Langlois's lighting arrangements were placed well below the level of the audience and more skilfully controlled.

He went on showing battle-pieces until 1857, his programmes varying less than those of other panorama and diorama makers not only because his pictures

Playbill advertising a diorama by Clarkson Stanfield shown at the Theatre Royal, Drury Lane, on February 4th, 1830. Dioramas were shown regularly at Drury Lane rather as some early movies were slipped into the programmes of variety theatres, to fill up gaps in the entertainment. (From the collection of Mrs. Beryl Perugia)

STANFIELD'S
GRAND LOCAL DIORAMA,

Embracing the most Picturesque Views of

WINDSOR and its VICINITY:

TOWN AND CASTLE OF WINDSOR,

From the Meadows above the Bridge.

The River, near Brocas Meadow. (Sunset)

ACROSS THE FIELDS TO

ETON, BY MOONLIGHT.

Windsor Great Park.

The CASTLE, from the Long Walk (Morning)

PLANTATIONS NEAR THE ROYAL LODGE.

VIRGINIA WATERS.

The Royal Pavilion

THE UPPER LAKE,

With the Frigate "VICTORINE."

THE DRY ARCH,

WITH ITS SPLENDID RUINS.

THE SERIES OF VIEWS TERMINATING WITH THE

MAGNIFICENT DISPLAY OF

THE FALLS

of

The Virginia Waters,

SEEN THROUGH

The FAIRY TEMPLE of LUMINARIA.—GRAND FINALE.

The New Grand Splendid Comic Christmas Pantomime, called

JACK IN THE BOX;

Or, Harlequin and the Princess of the Hidden Island, with

STANFIELD's MAGNIFICENT DIORAMA,

Will be repeated EVERY EVENING.

In rehearsal and will speedily be produced, Shakspeare's Historical Play of

HENRY THE FIFTH.

The Part of Henry the Fifth by Mr. KEAN,

(Being his 1st appearance in that Character)

Madame VESTRIS

Will perform this Evening, Saturday and Tuesday next.

☞ No ORDERS will be admitted.

To-morrow ...... The Brigand. Alessandro Massaroni (the Brigand Chief) Mr. Wallack.
And My Wife! What Wife?

seem to have been even more meticulously detailed than theirs but because his auditorium had to be freshly constructed for each new subject. At the time of the first International Paris Exhibition the palace of industry absorbed Langlois's rotunda and he set up another at the corner of the avenue des Champs-Élysées and the avenue d'Atun.

While it was being constructed, Langlois went off to the Crimea, taking with him a camera. On his return he produced two panoramas, *The Fall of Sebastopol* and *The Battle of Solferino*, in which photography was used for the first time as an integral part of a moving picture. From the Press notices of these shows it appears that Langlois probably employed a magic lantern behind the screen to project enlarged photographic images which mingled with those painted on the canvas. He had possibly relied on a magic lantern to create the figures of the Emperor and his companions in *The Burning of Moscow*.

Langlois died in 1870 and his vast paintings were all destroyed during the siege of Paris. But his use of photography in the making of moving pictures was followed up by MM. de Neuville and Détaille, who showed an entirely photographic *Battle of Rézonville* at the 1889 exhibition in which the effects of light were still further enhanced by means of tall cylindrical reflectors such as Kircher had brought into play more than two centuries previously to produce his *Ascension*. The *Battle* was awarded the *prix d'honneur* at the exhibition.

Dioramas and panoramas were still popular in London during the nineties. Over a million viewers were reported to have seen an ambitious programme featuring a journey from Niagara to London during the year in which it was shown by Philippoteaux at 10–22 York Street, Westminster. ('Electric light—Building properly warmed. Music. Colossal Panorama of the Great Falls. Admission 1s. Panoramic View of Southern cotton fields in full work. No extra charge.') And at Ashley Place, in 1890, a panorama of Waterloo was exhibited daily by Chev. P. Fleischer, the attraction of the entertainment being much heightened by the actual appearance of James Davey, 'Veteran and only known rank-and-file survivor of the great battle'.

Scarcely any of the immense number of panorama and diorama paintings executed during the nineteenth century survive. Depending, as they almost always did, on effects of artificial light, produced by means of lamps and gas jets, the great majority, like the buildings which housed them, ended in flames.

The Regent's Park Diorama, the only surviving building of its kind in London. The façade was designed by Nash to form the centre of the terrace in Park Square East. The rotunda and picture emplacements (invisible from the terrace) were the work of Augustus Charles Pugin and the engineer James Morgan. The word 'Diorama', originally on the facia, has been painted out

Among those destroyed by fire were the great diorama pictures of Daguerre and Bouton, all those of Gropius, and most of the panoramas designed by Stanfield and Roberts. Small toy panoramas were published by many print-sellers, including Spooner, Reeves and Sons, and Ackermann in London, and these have been preserved in museums and private collections. But they give little idea of the enchantment and splendour of the public entertainments.

The toy dioramas generally measure about 6 by 7½ in. inside a cardboard frame and consist of paper transparencies to be viewed by reflected and transmitted light. The panoramas take the form of a pictorial strip which can be gradually unrolled from a cylindrical box and shown through a cardboard slip. They vary in length from a few feet to several yards. The subjects are much the same as those of the full-size panoramas and dioramas; some are topographical, while others commemorate outstanding social or historical events. Among the many fascinating examples in the collection of J. R. Abbey is a continuous strip view of the north bank of the Thames seen from Albion Mill near Blackfriar's Bridge by Robert Barker, the inventor of the Panorama. Another celebrated miniature panorama in the same collection is *The Funeral of the Duke of Wellington* by Henry Alken and George Sala. *A View of Naples and Surrounding Scenery* by Henry Aston Barker, now in the possession of the Barnes brothers, was brought out in 1821 to coincide with the production of the large public panorama of the *View of Naples* exhibited at Barker's establishment in the Strand.

3

Far Eastern Shadows

Far in and out, above, about, below,
  'Tis nothing but a Magic Shadow-show,
  Played in a Box whose Candle is the Sun,
Round which we Phantom Figures come and go.
                    OMAR KHAYYÁM

EVERYONE has at some time experienced the uncanny power of shadows to bewitch and transform familiar objects. A flickering candle will set staid furniture lurching in grotesque silhouette to its own staccato rhythm; and with changing light the shadows attached to our own well-known bodies will assume unrecognizable shapes and proportions, broad and monstrous, humped and pygmy, drunkenly gesticulating, mocking every action. The shadow play is the art of imposing a formal discipline upon these capricious, insubstantial companions of mortality; and its simplest form is the hand-shadow entertainment.

In many of the Victorian books on games and pastimes which include instructions on the projection of hand shadows, and in Wilkie's picture of a father amusing the family circle by throwing upon the wall the favourite image of a rabbit, the hands and the light producing the silhouette are in full view of the spectators. As the hands open and close and the fingers bend and stretch, the head of a negro dissolves into that of a wolf, then turns into a goat, a goose, an elephant, a bald old man with drooping moustaches, and at last flutters out of sight in the likeness of a pigeon with outstretched wings. So lively, so full of character, are the shadows that the operator's movements soon cease to attract the eye absorbed only by the dream-like spectacle.

47

This mysterious effect of autonomous movement is enhanced and can be subjected to far greater control when the hands are replaced by cut-out puppets, themselves scarcely more than shadows, flinging their shapes not on to the wall but upon the back of an illuminated screen which divides the audience and the image from the showman. In the wide range of its subject-matter, which, like that of the cinema, can be described as illustrated narrative rather than drama, and in its consistent use of the animated projected image, this form of shadow play is more akin to the film than any of the varieties of moving pictures which diverted earlier ages. Its brilliant exploitation of the visually fantastic and extravagant points the direction in which the real opportunities of the movies, so often lost in the pursuit of naturalism, would seem to lie.

The origins of the shadow show are obscure, although scholars agree that it first developed either in India or in China. A Chinese authority, Sun Kai-ti, says that the shades were invented during the Tang period in about 900, but were not established until the eleventh century. Tradition places the invention as far back as the reign of the Han Emperor Wu Ti (140–86 B.C.) when a necromancer is supposed to have conjured up the vision of a departed concubine who appeared before her royal lover in the shape of a silhouette on a screen. Even if this tale, interesting for its similarity to the stories told about magic mirrors, be unreliable, it suggests that there was a connection between the shadow play and the supernatural, and this is borne out by what is known of the art in other Far Eastern lands. In Java, as in India, the shadow theatre was part of religious ritual and was believed to be a means of warding off evil, while in Siam, or Thailand, as it is now called, the shades were exhibited only during the celebrations which accompanied the cremation of the dead.

Anyone accustomed to think of shadows as black or varying degrees of grey must be astonished by his first sight of Chinese puppets. These paper-thin, elegant figures are brightly painted in translucent colours so that they glow through the screen like sunlit stained glass. This effect is often heightened by designs composed of a number of small planes, hardly more naturalistic than a Cubist picture, covering all but the flesh parts. These are usually cut away except for an incredibly fine outline, so that faces and hands shine white and clear on the screen in striking contrast to the iridescent clothing. It is said that the earliest shadow figures were made of transparent bone or horn, but those seen today in museum collections, or in China where the showman still summons them to active life, are cut from the finest leather—sheepskin in the southern provinces, and skin from the donkey's belly, almost as colourless and crystalline as glass, in the north.

Most of the shades are in complete profile, though sometimes the head may be turned towards the spectator; they are about 12 in. high and are jointed by means of silk knots at the shoulders, elbows, and hips; they also have hinged waists and flexible hands. The head is often rather large in proportion to the body, with the features much exaggerated. Different heads can be fitted in turn to the same figure, by means of a slot in the collar, to indicate reincarnations and transformations. To the neck and to each hand are attached thin iron pins 3 to 4 in. long, and these are inserted into smooth, light reeds affording a grip for the manipulator's fingers. He operates from a felt-covered wooden shelf behind a screen measuring from 4 to 5 ft. across, made of linen or mulberry paper and stretched between bamboo poles.

A fully equipped Chinese shadow company includes an orchestra of from three to five musicians who between them play some twelve or fourteen distinct instruments: cymbals, the gong, zither, tambour, and the bamboo pipes with their thin, eerie treble. The musicians support the show with improvised strains which quicken or lag according to the mood of the commentary.

A showman who was working in Peking just before the Second World War operated with one hundred and fifty figures and more than a thousand detachable heads. His shades included officials of all kinds: emperors and their concubines, servitors, sages and hermits, gods and goddesses, buffoons and palace ladies, and demons distinguished by their devils' masks. There was the Ox-headed Demon, the God of Thunder with cruelly beaked upper lip, and the sly Fox Demon, a beautiful woman with a fox on her head-dress. Still more like apparitions than these fabulous creatures were the tall emaciated Suicide Ghosts, drooping and diaphanous. Their eyes bulged and stared and their long, black, lolling tongues showed that they had hanged themselves, the suicide method most approved by the Chinese. They served the Lord of Hell as messengers to possible recruits to the infernal regions and appear to have been numerous, for theirs are the heads most often found amongst the dust and litter of the recent past.

There are several centres in China famous for the production of shadow figures: Liang-hsiang-hsien, about a hundred miles west of Peking, and the small town of Lanchow, where the shades surpass all others for delicacy, durability, and originality, its reputation resembling that of Epinal in Alsace for the superior manufacture of paper toys. Yu-t'ien, about two hundred and fifty miles from Peking, was associated earlier in the present century with Liu Chen-yin, one of the most outstanding of all shadow artists, and Peking was the home of two more celebrated craftsmen of the same period, Li-Hsiang and Lan Hsaio-shan. The names of the master cutters of the more distant past, like those of the great popular designers in every other sphere, have hardly ever been recorded.

The plays performed by the Chinese showmen can no more be ascribed to particular authors than the shades themselves. They reached the form in which we know them today through a long process of development, moulded by tradition and by the idiosyncrasies of generations of operators; and they continue to change and grow. When the Russian puppet-master Obraztsov attended the All Chinese Festival of Puppet and Shadow Theatres in 1955 he found that many of the stock legendary pieces contained allusions to contemporary events and that a series of new fable-plays had been added to the shadow repertoire.

The traditional themes fall into several groups: religious, legendary, historic, satiric, comic, and domestic. Many of the pieces, like some of the early films, are intended to be shown in serial form. One long historic cycle, *The Beggar Emperor*, consists of eight plays, characteristically entitled *Throwing the Ball*, *The Casting out of the Son-in-law*, *The Hand Shaking*, *The Farewell in the Tile Factory*, *The Second Farewell in the Tile Factory*, *The Departure from the Tile Factory*, *The Wild Goose as a Messenger of Love*, and *The Return to the Imperial Palace*. The texts, published in translation at Yiu Chow in 1915, surprisingly reticent and illumined by flashes of poetry and humour, are the counterparts of the exquisite figures that play them out.

But this series seems to be less popular than *The Wars of the Three Kingdoms* and *The White Serpent*. Both these sequences provide the showman with opportunities for improvisation and embroidery and are full of the marvellous transformations and prodigious feats in which lies the whole strength of the shadow show. In the piece called *On the Fen min shan Mountains*, for instance, when the white-haired but stout-hearted Chao Yün offers to defeat the enemy single-handed or forfeit his life, the operator makes him catch the arrow launched against him, notch the shaft in his own bow, and bring down a couple of birds with a trial shot before transfixing his foe; or, if the audience demands it, he will cut off the heads of four bold generals with one sweep of his sword, leap, as only a shadow can, across a torrent to fell a fifth, and stand ready to face an entire army. In the *White Serpent* play *The Flooding of the Monastery of the Golden Mountain* the serpent goes to battle with the priests in order to win back her husband who has been lured into the monastery. When she challenges the abbot he hurls down his staff, which in its descent changes into a dragon lusting to fight the intruder, but instantly water demons come to the snake's aid and fifteen great fountains shoot up, threatening to engulf the monastery. The abbot, strengthened by Buddha, covers his opponent with his alms-bowl and the sorceress is forced to flee in her true guise, that of a gigantic, terrifying reptile.

The essentially visual character of the Chinese shadow show is manifest not only in heroic and supernatural pieces of the kind just described but in simple plays in which there is no real climax or dénouement and only the flimsiest strand of narrative. Such is the Ming shadow show *Picking up the Jade Bracelet*. The heroine, Sun Yu-chiao, the daughter of an indigent widow, is sitting at her embroidery when the play opens. It is spring and all her movements indicate that she is restless and cannot concentrate. As she laments her lot, the young and handsome Fu Peng passes by. He is instantly captivated by her charms and, hoping to win her favour, places a jade bracelet on the threshold of her house. Yu-chiao walks with small quick steps to the door and hovers about the bracelet, the inhumanly supple yet perceptibly jerky movements of her shadow-puppet limbs and head expressing a long-drawn-out struggle between desire and propriety which Fu Peng watches from a distance. At last Yu-chiao succumbs to the temptation, picks up the bracelet, and vanishes into the house. An old crone who has witnessed everything now comes forward and calls to the young girl. Yu-chiao comes to her door once more and the old woman persuades her to confess what has happened and to admit that she would be grateful for the services of a matchmaker. She then hobbles off with one of Yu-chiao's tiny shoes as a pledge to Fu Peng. That is all.

A description by Lafcadio Hearn of a shadow show he saw in 1907 in the courtyard of the temple at Matsue on the occasion of a great night festival suggests that the Japanese shadow theatre closely resembled that of the Chinese.

The dialogue was spoken by an invisible person, the actors and scenery were softly luminous shades that reminded Hearn of magic-lantern projections he had seen as a boy, except that they were endowed with uncanny life and were so compelling that he felt as though he were confronted by some strange goblin vision.

The forms taken by the shadow show elsewhere in the Far East are very different. It is necessary only to glimpse some of the richly decorative, intense figures of the Javanese and Indian shades hanging inertly in our public museums, or to read a page or two of the few texts translated by members of the Indian Civil Service or by Georg Jacob, to be carried away by the wild exuberance and unbounded fantasy of a spirit remote indeed from the delicate poetry and gentle reticence of the Chinese shadows. And when reading the plays it is impossible not to be struck by the emphasis on effects which would be entirely out of place on the stage and could be successfully engineered only on the screen.

Indian and Javanese shadow shows are crowded with grotesque beings, with hordes of monkeys, with multi-headed, many-armed monsters; they rely on staggering transformation scenes and on splendid processions and celestial visions, all of which are spectacular rather than dramatic. And many of the plays open with effects reminiscent of those favoured by Loutherbourg and the diorama makers. The *Pandavabhyndaya*, for instance, begins with a sunrise which gradually banishes the lingering darkness and mists of night and reveals a cloud of bees hovering about the bursting buds of lotus flowers. A moment of peace before the romantic, almost incoherent, story unfolds of Draupad's birth from the smoke of incense, her choice of a mate, and her elaborate wedding celebrations. Again, in the *Ramabhyndaya*, Sita has to prove her loyalty to Rama by undergoing a trial by fire. As she is committed to the flames, a company of deities draws near on airborne chariots, while the fire god Vahui rises from the blaze and leads Sita to safety. Then Rama's faithful companion, the monkey king, announces Rama's return to Ayodhya (Oudh). An embassy places the insignia of kingship before Rama, he is crowned with great ceremony, and a rain of blossom falls from heaven. There is no dramatic unity and scarcely any connection between the first and second halves of the play.

Some authorities believe that the Indian shadow show is more ancient than that of China, and that a cave in Sargura, Bengal, was used as a shadow theatre during the second century B.C. Their assumption rests on an enigmatical

Three aspects of a sheet from a mid-nineteenth-century book of moving pictures, the subject of each of which changes into its opposite as the tab at the bottom of the page is pulled. These photographs show three stages in the transformation of Earth to Air

EARTH.   AIR.

MAN, though so feeble at his birth,
Explores the lowest depths of EARTH;
Balloons enable him to dare
The lofty regions of the AIR.

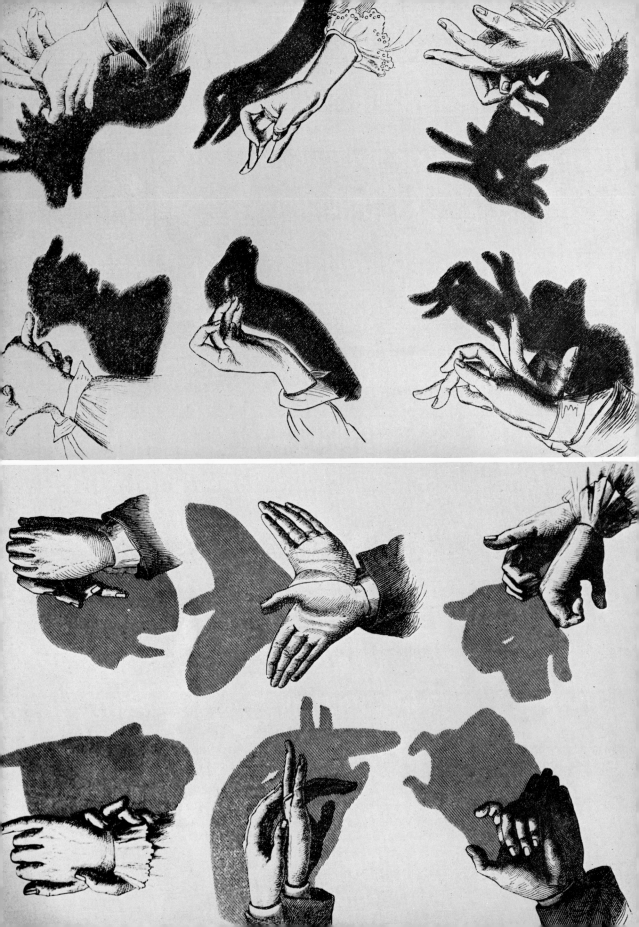

inscription and has never been proved. Georg Jacob suggests that the oldest of the Indian shadow plays is the so-called *Hanumun Nataka*, which originated before 859 and deals with the legend of Rama in its entirety, taking its title from the monkey king Hanumun, a favourite character.

The great national epics, the *Ramayana* and the *Mahabharata*, provide the subjects of most of the known texts, but Jacob translated a Jain religious piece by the poet Meghaprabhacarya, the original text of which was published in Bhavnagar in 1918, and which combines the spectacular quality of the traditional Indian shadow show with the presentation of Jain ideals. The title, *Dharmabhyndaya*, means 'The Way to Fulfilment' or 'The True Awakening', and the main character of the play, King Dacarnabhadra, is led by various stages to a state of indifference to all earthly pleasures. As he sits on his throne, fanned by fair maidens and surrounded by his court, he receives news that the founder of Jainism, the great Mahavira, has come down to earth. At once he leaves his palace, mounts his elephant, and sets out with a splendid retinue to do homage to the 'Liberator from the Ocean of Being'. All the gods (no more, according to Jainism, than the relics of a poetic myth) are also hastening to acknowledge Mahavira. The chief of them, Indra, rides on Airavana to greet the saint, accompanied by a host of fabulous beings. The king, carried away by his emotions, utters the Jain vow and is instantly changed into a monk. Indra bows before the new saint as well as before Mahavira then returns with pomp to Paradise, where he is entertained by a marvellous pantomime, full of oriental magic.

The shades by means of which these exotic Indian pieces are unfolded are not articulated at the joints like the Chinese figures, but are simple shapes cut out of light-coloured transparent skin, outlined in black, and decorated with bright red and blue stains. The Siamese figures and subjects are closely related to them; but they consist not only of single shadows, the more modern Nang Talung, but of entire scenes, the Nang Lung, which are thrown, a little more than life-size, on to a gigantic screen behind which flares a mighty open fire.

A fine collection of these composite figures, some of which have unfortunately been gnawed by rats, can be seen at the Munich Ethnographical Museum. One of the most impressive shows Hanuman bearing a whole peak of the Himalayas to a field of battle in order to restore the fallen heroes with the herbs growing on the mountain slopes. This vast group picture is drawn on

Hand shadows

buffalo hide with perforated outlines, with the images enclosed in a complicated ornamental setting. The flesh parts are cut away so that they appear shining white on the screen. During the performance two speakers explained the scene while as many as from eight to twenty persons moved the great silhouette slowly to and fro by means of two supports. Such spectacles were shown, as I have said, only at cremation ceremonies, and it is thought that they represent an early stage in the development of the shadow play, as did the whole method of presentation, with the recital or reading from the national epics taking the place of dialogue. The word *Nang*, it is interesting to note, which means leather, is the name by which the cinema is known today in Thailand.

Until recently there was a cumbersome form of shadow show in Java, the so-called Wayang Beber, which had much in common with the Siamese group scenes and which must have been rather like the European panoramas. It consisted of large sheets of cloth more than two yards long and about one and a half feet wide, on which scenes and figures were delineated with perforated outlines and painted. They were illuminated from behind and slowly unrolled from a wooden bar while the invisible dalang, or showman, gave a commentary in a monotonous voice to the sound of bell music. The theme was generally the story of a prince and his legendary adventures; it occupied about seven rolls and took one and a half hours to show.

But the most developed and characteristic type of Javanese shadow play, still popular today, belongs to quite a different tradition. Technically it seems to derive from Chinese rather than Indian example. The method of jointing the figures and manipulating them by means of rods is similar, though generally it is only the arms of Javanese shades which are articulated. And in all but this matter of technique they are a race apart: haunting, inhuman creatures with bird-like profiles, immensely long, attenuated arms, and strange filigree decoration enveloping their lower limbs and encrusting their heads like flowering moss. Made of dried, smoothed buffalo hide, they look, when they are out of the hands of the dalang and when, as so often, their bright colours are dimmed by age and neglect, like shrivelled mummies or wizened bats intently awaiting the fall of darkness to spring into spectral life. Hanging motionless against a wall, or locked behind the glass of a museum case, they pulse with the same dynamic force as that which emanates from the similarly conventionalized Scythian bronzes or Celtic illuminations.

Unlike the Indian, Siamese, and early Balinese figures, which are often shown full-face or in half-profile, and are rendered with convincing realism even when they wield four arms, the heads and feet of the Javanese puppets are always in profile, while their bodies, and very often their eyes, are frontal; and these bodies are transformed into decorative curves and spirals. The convention is due in part to the fact that the Javanese, as Mohammedans, were prohibited from making direct likenesses of human beings. And the use of shapes suggesting birds' heads may have originally been a deliberate allusion to the belief that the souls of the departed took the form of birds; this seems all the more likely when it is remembered that the shadows were at first associated with the dead.

The earlier the figures, the more stylized they tend to be. Although there is mention of the wajang or shadow show in the eleventh century in Java, the earliest known shade, now in the Munich Ethnographical Museum, dates from the seventeenth century and came from the collection of a Jesuit priest who died in 1732. It represents Banuwati, the consort of Duryodhanas, but bears scarcely any relation to the human form. The body is cased in the most intricate filigree work from which the forward-jutting sharp black profile on its snaky neck and the thin expressive arms emerge like the head and limbs of a beetle.

The later and more frequently encountered figures are naked to the waist, and the ornament is confined to the head and clothing. They all conform to distinct types moulded by tradition. A thin nose, flat brow, narrow slanting eyes, and compressed lips indicate high rank and intellectual power; a short thick nose, a rounded brow, and broad mouth signify physical strength and nobility of spirit; half-closed eyes suggest the peace of fulfilment; monsters, demons, and monkey-figures are all shown with snarling open mouths and pointed teeth, while the hair is coiled into a crescent-shaped horn. But there are endless subtle variations on each prescribed type; each vigorous shade impresses its own strong personality on the spectator, and together they form a bewildering, intensely vital assembly of gods and goddesses, heroes, ancestors, chieftains, warriors and hunters, kings and princes, fearsome giants, twice the size of both men and gods, sorcerers and legions of demons; and all are mocked, when the power and passion of the action are too great to be borne, by the grotesque clowns, Semar and his sons, Gareng, Petruk, and Bagong. The stories they enact are taken, like the Indian shadow plays, from the *Ramayana* and the *Mahabharata* and also from the purely Javanese *Manik Maja*,

55

and are as fantastic as the figures themselves, full of abductions, sorcery, heroic battles, demon lovers, and incredible transformations.

Though only the shoulders and elbows of the Javanese shadow puppet are articulated, the whole figure throbs with life when the dalang manipulates the horn rods attached to the hands. The main support by which he grasps the puppet consists of a piece of cleft horn running from the tip of the head-dress on both sides of the figure, following its sinuous form and emphasizing the design with its bold line. It ends in a point which can be fitted into the soft pith of a banana stem at the base of the stage when the shadow is at rest. The dalang uses a bronze hanging lamp in the form of a weird bird to project the shadows, and his large screen is stretched on a bamboo structure.

The play is accompanied by an orchestra known as the gamelan, some twenty to twenty-five players performing on gongs and rows of small metal discs struck with a hammer. A German traveller, Wilhelm Geiger, gives an interesting account of this music in a book written during the thirties, *Unter Tropischer Sonne*. It owes its unearthly, melancholy character to the gradation of the tones not as in European music merely into halves but into eighths. It sounds, Geiger says, like a deep syncopated tintinnabulation, endlessly improvising on a few themes and most skilfully adapted to the movements of the shades. Noises off stage are produced in a traditional manner: the dalang places the box in which he keeps his figures within reach of his right foot, and when the clash of arms or the roar of a storm is to be heard he vigorously kicks two or three metal discs attached to the box.

The effect of the music, mournful and yet stirring, of the dalang's voice, changing with each character, of the flickering lamplight and the ghostly, swiftly moving shadows with their exaggerated gestures and the broken patterns cast by the filigree work of their fabulous forms, is entirely magical. A recent visitor describes how a large audience at a performance in Djokjakarta, among them whole families of young children, sat spellbound all through the night from 9 p.m. till 5 a.m., the usual duration of a play, cheering the silhouettes of Sita and Rama, acclaiming the monkey king and collapsing with laughter when the pot-bellied Semar flew across the screen.

The Javanese shadow plays were originally designed for male audiences only and the men were permitted to sit on either side of the screen to watch either the shadows or the figures that cast them. Later, women were admitted to the audience, but they were allowed to see nothing but the shadows. It is because the puppets themselves are part of the show that they are often so elaborately coloured. The torso, arms, and legs are gilded, the face, hair, and beard are painted black, while the patterned filigree work is coloured red, white, dark blue, black, and gold. The oriental scholar Carl Hagemann gives a vivid description of a show seen from behind the screen. So smoothly and quietly did the dalang work, that his presence was utterly forgotten and Hagemann was conscious of nothing but the puppets. 'They were intended to represent spirits', he writes, 'and they *were* spirits.' A Javanese member of the audience told him, 'When we watch the Wayang figures fighting we see the fire flashing from their eyes.' Hagemann stresses the religious aspect of the performance, less apparent now than at the time he was writing—the second decade of the present century. The dalang first got his shades into order and then made an offering of fruit, rice, flowers, little flags, and candles at an altar by the screen. Next, like Cellini's Sicilian priest, he lit a pile of sweet-smelling herbs which sent up clouds of fragrant smoke to excite the senses of the audience and prepare them for the marvels they were about to witness.

Though still very much alive, the Javanese shadow show has inevitably declined with the influence of the West and the attempts of a rapidly growing population to adapt itself to modern industrial life. But the cinema theatre, which now rivals the shadow play throughout the Far East as a popular entertainment, far from being antagonistic to the ancient tradition, must be regarded as another form of it. In China, Japan, India, and Indonesia the legitimate theatre was a later development than the shadow play and the actors based their stylized movements and costumes on those of the shades. The image on the flat screen seemed more eloquent, more significant, than the three-dimensional, flesh-and-blood actor. The symbolic power of the shadow, universally felt, but only rarely acknowledged in the West in seldom-read works—of which Chamisso's romantic story of Peter Schlehmil is a memorable example—is deeply woven into the fabric of Far Eastern culture. It is therefore not surprising that the most impressive and successful of Japanese films should have been based on legendary themes and that they should have an obvious affinity with the little shadow play described by Lafcadio Hearn. And anyone acquainted with the characters and material of Indian shadow shows would immediately recognize the chaotic, mythological, fantastically spectacular films made earlier in the century by the Shadra Film Company in Bombay as a modern development of a native tradition.

So natural is the medium to the Indians that they have even used it, quite unself-consciously, in the service of religion. Just as the shadow show celebrates the gods of the Buddhist and Brahmin hierarchies, so the film conjured up the divinities of the new religion from the West, Christianity. Curt Moreck, in a fascinating book on the sociological aspects of the cinema, reports that when he was in Calcutta in 1908 the cinema was regularly used in the churches there as part of the ritual. After the priest had intoned his final Amen, a single choir boy would sing a hymn while every light was slowly extinguished and the windows were shuttered. Clouds of incense bemused the senses of the congregation, and then suddenly through the smoke a colossal figure of Christ was flung on to a screen. The whole scene of Christ walking on the waters was shown in vivid detail: mountainous seas threatened to engulf the worshippers, the pallid moon shone fitfully through ragged clouds and cast a metallic glow on the giant, striding figure, his white, billowing robe, and the terrified Peter. If any proof were needed of the direct kinship of the film and the magic practices of the priests of antiquity and of Kircher with his projection of the Ascension, Moreck's account provides it.

4

Karagöz

All life is controlled by the Master who remains behind the screen;
Surely thou believest not that these little figures move of their own
free will?

BAKI

IT SEEMS at first a far cry from the stylized figures and the heroic themes of
the oriental shadow play to the farcical naturalistic show which developed in
Europe. Even the simpler, more domestic, of the Far Eastern plays, such as
Picking up the Jade Bracelet, appear to have nothing in common with rollicking
pieces like *The Broken Bridge*, which became the stock play of both street and
fashionable showmen in France and England. But a strong tradition of
boisterous humour was nurtured in Turkey from whence there are many
indications that it infiltrated into Europe.

The shadow show is usually said to have spread to Turkey from the Far
East through Persia, but the first mention of the art in Turkey occurs in the
journal of the seventeenth-century traveller Thévenot. By this time any
resemblance there may have been between the Turkish entertainment and
the oriental convention had vanished, and the former had assumed a slapstick
comic character and had taken the name of its principal figure, the clown
Karagöz or Black Eye. He has a curious history. This merry Andrew, stupid,
naive, more boastful than Punch, and wonderfully ready with his tongue,
commemorates a worthy statesman called Qaraqusch who died early in the
thirteenth century. The friend and counsellor of Saladin, he had a jealous rival,
a certain Ibn Mammati, who lampooned him in a political satire. The squib

became the subject of a popular ballad and eventually produced the shadow puppet Karagöz, who has nothing in common with his illustrious progenitor but his name.

The texts of a large number of Turkish shadow plays have been published and translated, mostly into German, and the wide variations in different transcriptions of the same subjects indicate that much of the effect of these rapidly moving entertainments must always have depended, even more than in the case of the Javanese shows, on the nimble wit and spontaneity of the showman, or hajaldschy, as he is called in Turkey, who grafts fresh banter and new jokes on to the traditional material as he goes along and brings his hero's exploits right up to date. The modern Karagöz travels by air and has already begun to explore outer space.

All the plays follow a certain pattern. Each character enters singing a short song, and in a prologue spoken by Karagöz's companion and foil, Hacivad, we are told that the show is more than an entertainment: the figures shadow forth the design of the 'master showman of the universe' and those who seek the truth which lies behind reality will find it on the screen. Then Karagöz emerges from his house to meet Hacivad and a lively dialogue ensues. Karagöz wilfully misunderstands all that his correct, pedantic friend says, he makes coarse puns on the foreign expressions with which Hacivad loves to pepper his sentences, and rhymes solemn pronouncements with nonsense.

'What a misfortune, Karagöz,' says Hacivad, 'that you were born such an ass and have never been anything else but an ass.'

K. What's that, you rascal? Because you were born an ass do you expect to turn into a mule? (gives him a crack with his cudgel)
H. Ah, my dear Karagöz, you aren't to blame, it's all due to your upbringing.

K. You really think that accounts for everything?
H. There can be no doubt.

K. Then I'm absolutely prohibited from spending a penny from now on.
H. Why, how's that, Karagöz?

Shadows cast by three oriental puppets of dried buffalo skin, painted and gilded. *Above:* Arjuna the mythical hero, and *below:* Hanuman the monkey king, both from Java; *top right:* Civa, from Bali. The shadows are opaque except for the patterned perforations. (From the collection of Mr. George Speaight)

Shadows cast by four Turkish puppets. The figures are of painted translucent camel skin and throw coloured shadows. *Above:* The hero Karagöz (*right*) from whom the Turkish shadow theatre takes its name, with Celebi, a foppish young man. *Below:* The Zenne, the name given to all the female characters in the Karagöz world, and Beberuhi the dwarf

K. If I can't take anything in, how can anything come out?
H. How I detest such nonsensical sophistical speciousness.

K. I can't bear such reprehensible, prolifical facetiousness either.
H. Don't talk such twaddle.

K. See the stork waddle!
H. Ne parle pas à tort et à travers.

K. The parlour bar's for taking the air.

This sort of talk usually ends with the two friends confiding to each other that neither has any money and resolving to set up some kind of business. It is always Karagöz who does the work, while Hacivad brings him customers or patrons. He becomes a scribe, a ferryman, a schoolmaster, a poet, a clairvoyant, a doctor, an interpreter; he even professes to cure the insane. And always Karagöz lays about him with his cudgel and sets everyone by the ears with his foolish antics. He will suddenly send the contents of his chamber-pot flying across the screen, then set it on his head instead of the hat, shaped like a Victorian jelly mould, which is his customary wear; he will boastfully climb a haunted tree, cut off the branch upon which he is sitting, and come hurtling to the ground, or he will try to separate two quarrelsome cronies by banging them on the head with an outsize watering-can, swinging it with such impetuous rhythm that his own head is included in the banging.

Certain characters tend to recur in the plays, especially those representing racial types: a Persian in a tall lambskin hat; an Anatolian woodcutter with an axe on his shoulder, a fierce eye, a pronounced nose, and a thick black beard; a dandified Frenchman in waisted jacket, tapering trousers, and a peaked or top hat; an Arab in flowing robes; an Armenian in a long skirt; a Jew with unmistakable profile and supplicating gesture. Street-hawkers and water-carriers are also among the stock characters, together with a rich young lover, Celebi, dressed in the latest mode, and a sailor from Trebizond with a scarf round his head and an ingratiating smile.

In addition to the figures, the Turkish shadow show is enlivened by the most charming set-pieces, always included in the cast listed at the beginning of published scripts. There is a fortified gateway, a bath-house, a palace,

Karagöz's own humble abode, an arbour surrounded by flowering bushes, and an Ali Baba vat to hide one of Mrs. Karagöz's lovers, all designed in much the same large, robust, naive spirit as the ornament on early Staffordshire pottery.

The Turkish figures are smaller than the Javanese puppets, usually about 9 in. high, although one of the characters, a dwarf, is smaller still, not more than 5 or 6 in. tall. They are made of camel-skin which has been treated until it is softly translucent like a piece of very fine jade or palest cornelian still salty from the sea. The forms are firmly outlined in black and richly coloured, the faces a warm flesh, the hair jet, the clothing, often patterned with motifs like those on Turkish pots, deep glowing red, plum, apple-green, cobalt, and yellow. This fine colour, like that of the Chinese shades, shines through the screen when the figures are in action.

All the puppets are in complete profile and for the most part are jointed only at the waist and sometimes at the knees. Occasionally the head also is articulated and in some instances a figure is provided with two heads, one hanging down and the other in position, and in a transformation scene these will be quickly reversed. The Karagöz figure of the nineteenth and twentieth centuries is usually given one long arm jointed at the shoulder and elbow, and one of the characters in *The Boat*, a toper with a gun, also has a long, jointed arm. This long arm is deliciously eloquent; with it Karagöz will cross himself on the bosom with an effect which always produces laughter from an audience very fond of using this gesture. But in general the Turkish shades are remarkable for their extraordinarily short arms, held close to the body, and for their minute feet. They are manipulated by means of one or, occasionally, two horizontal rods fitted into little sockets. The waist joints are loose and when the figures are in action they dart about the screen with all the skipping, bowing, swaying, jerking movement of the spritely dialogue. They have none of the elegance of the Chinese puppets and none of the intense, romantic poetry of the Javanese silhouettes, but they are extraordinarily lively and convincing with their large almond eyes—the whites of which are cut away so that the pupils appear startlingly black upon the screen—and the caricature-like treatment of the large heads.

Originally the shadows were projected by the uncertain light of torches and the performance was accompanied by several musicians playing drums and flutes. Now the action is usually supported by gramophone music, except for the songs, which are rendered by voice and guitar. Modern electricity illumines the long, narrow screen with such brilliancy as to tire the eyes, rather as the early cinema is said to have done.

Karagöz's whole personality often reminds us of Punch. Like the English puppet he has a hump, he is very ready with his cudgel, though less savage, and he is decidedly amorous even if he is not often successful. Mrs. Karagöz nags, loses no chance of putting her husband to shame, and is frequently unfaithful, and Karagöz never subdues her as Punch does Mrs. Punch. The kinship of the two puppets probably comes from their common ancestry, for both have descended from the antique Circurricus and the Neapolitan Pulcinelle. Karagöz also has something in common with the Harlequin of the Commedia dell'Arte. One of the coarsest of the Arabic texts, in which the hero is made to believe he is a pregnant woman, exactly corresponds to one of the stock pieces of the Commedia dell'Arte where Harlequin finds himself in the same ridiculous and touching situation. The play in which Karagöz sets up as a scribe turns up in Germany as part of the repertoire of the Kasperltheater, and the episode where he tries to become a schoolmaster provided the material for one of the most popular French shadow shows during the nineteenth century. Karagöz himself, with his black beard and cudgel, appears incongruously among the silhouettes for a toy shadow show on a Victorian sheet published by Clarke; and he even travelled as far afield as America, for Winifred Mills saw his jolly outline in 1938 on a little screen in a New York coffee-house.

Karagöz dominated the shadow play in Egypt, in North Africa, and in Greece, changing his name to Karagyooz, Karakusch, and Karagkiozis, and it was therefore almost inevitable that he should influence the shadow play in Europe. A description given by a Frenchman in a popular magazine of 1872 of a show he attended in Algiers reveals definite affinities between the Karagöz spectacle and the shadow theatre which played such a prominent role in Parisian life during the last quarter of the nineteenth century. The Algerian performance, like all the Arabic Karagöz pieces, dispensed with the traditional Turkish prologue. Caragheuse, as the French narrator calls him, appeared on the screen at once in conversation with a Jew who spoke in dialect. The Jew was succeeded by a Christian and a widow, and all three were mimicked and made the butt of Karagöz's jokes; he next encountered a magician and was changed into an ass, as in one of the Turkish plays; and finally he was involved in a naval battle and the whole play ended with a grand procession of gods and men, tall, short, fat, and thin, viziers, vagabonds, soldiers and sultans, demons and dervishes. The element of magic mingled with rough comedy was common in the European shadow play during the eighteenth and nineteenth centuries, while processions in various forms became a speciality of the French shadow theatre.

Karagöz was still popular in the cafés and bazaars of Istanbul and Ankara when Hellmut Ritter, the translator of many of the traditional plays, visited those towns some twenty years ago. A number of clever showmen were still working at that time; Ritter mentions in particular a post-office official called Hayali Kücük Ali who operated in Ankara, and Acikgöz, a glazier, at Istanbul. Kücük Ali died in 1959, but he has been succeeded by three or four of his pupils. Yet performances appear to be given less and less frequently. Public shows take place only during the carnival month of Ramadan, and the entertainment is otherwise confined to the home, the showmen going round rather as professional conjurers attend private parties.

In Athens, on the other hand, Karagöz is very much alive. Just before and during the war years the great showman Mollas extended and enriched the material to include Greek historical pieces. His stage was much larger than that of the Turks, about 20 ft. wide and $4\frac{1}{2}$ ft. high, and his figures, too, were larger, averaging 2 ft. in height, and more varied. Mollas used iron rods instead of wooden ones to manipulate the shades and he worked in a permanently established theatre, in the open air in summer and indoors during the winter months. His gifted contemporaries, Markos Xanthos and Konstantin Manos, used similar methods; and their work is being carried on today by Y. Charidimos, son of another famous showman, Christos Charidimos.

In the Greek plays Karagöz and his slapstick are shown only as a curtain-raiser, though this may well last for more than half an hour. The main feature, going on for about four hours, is concerned with some purely Greek theme such as the struggle for independence, in which a great bearded Turk called Aly Pasha, celebrated for his terrible rages, plays a conspicuous part, moving very expressively with a backward inclination of the body. The Greek showmen make use of a device not known in the traditional Karagöz entertainment by which the characters suddenly change the direction in which they face. Their shadows lose focus, momentarily disappear, then re-emerge in reverse.

Anyone who has watched Karagöz and laughed at his pranks and frolics, his monkey tricks, mimicry, and horseplay, will at once recognize his kinship with the clowns of the celluloid.

5

The Chinese Shades

It was invented over there with the Chinese, and some travellers
went over there and see them doing it, and they come over here and
tell us about it. They didn't do it as we do, you know. As for doing
pieces, we lick them out of the field. Them only did the shadows, we
do a piece with 'em.

MAYHEW'S GALANTEE SHOWMAN

THE name by which the shadow show was generally known in Europe at
the time of its greatest popularity, *ombres chinoises*, suggests that the enthusiasm
for this form of entertainment which developed during the eighteenth and
nineteenth centuries was part of the fashionable craze for chinoiserie. But
Georg Jacob heard Turks in Istanbul refer to the Karagöz plays as 'the Chinese
shades' at the beginning of this century, and it was almost certainly Turkish and
not Chinese influence which fostered the growth of the shadow play in the
West. This, together with the taste for the silhouette, was responsible for the
plainly profiled naturalistic shades of France, England, and Germany. As so
often during the period when the term 'chinoiserie' first came into use, the
late seventeenth and early eighteenth centuries, it referred vaguely to the Orient
in general.

The shadow show must have been known in Europe before this time, for
Ben Jonson concludes his *The Tale of a Tub* with a shadow play. It is not at all
clear from the text exactly how the play was performed. Ben Jonson's showman,
Master In and In, is intended as a caricature of Inigo Jones, and the show he
arranges satirizes the court masques in which Jones and Jonson had collaborated,
Inigo Jones supplying the décor and costumes, Ben Jonson the text. The poet's

part had been overlooked in the handsome tributes paid to the visual beauties of the masques, and Jonson's revenge was to make the shadow show in *The Tale of a Tub* the meanest possible entertainment. This is how In and In describes his preparations:

'Now, Sir, this Tub I will have capt with paper,
A fine oil'd lanthorne paper that we use.

.   .   .   .   .

Which in it doth contain the light to the business,
And shall with every vapour of the candle
Drive all the motions of our matter about
As we present them.'

Mr. George Speaight makes the ingenious suggestion that the figures were applied to a round shade set up on top of the tub and made to revolve in the heat of wax candles burning inside them. I visualize the tub on its side with the paper-capped top or screen facing the spectators, the puppets being manipulated inside the open-bottomed cask and continually changing shape in the unsteady candlelight. This seems to accord with the image Ben Jonson gives of the showman drawing aside the curtain in front of the assembled audience to disclose 'the top of the tub', with a speaker standing in front with a silver-tipped wand to interpret the five scenes or 'motions'. This may not have been a characteristic shadow show of the time, but its inclusion in *The Tale of a Tub* at least proves the existence of the shades in England at the beginning of the seventeenth century.

Shadow showmen from Italy must have been performing in this country during the early years of the following century, for in his *Memoirs of Bartholomew Fair* Henry Morley records that in 1737 'Italian shadows by the best Masters from Italy, and which have not been seen here these twenty years', could be enjoyed at 'Hallam's Great Booth over against the Hospital Gate'. Italian shadow shows are reported to have been given at Danzig in 1683 and at Frankfurt in 1692, and a certain Chiarini gave a performance of *ombres chinoises* at Hamburg in the 1740's. From the description of the figures it is

Model of a shadow-play booth on the pavement outside the basement shadow theatre of Xapidhamos in Athens

evident that they were operated in an entirely different manner from the oriental puppets. Their hinged joints were attached to strings to the ends of which rings were tied, the rings fitting on to the fingers of the showman, who manipulated them as if he were playing a piano.

Later in the eighteenth century, in December 1775, a Frenchman called Ambroise, who had already shown in Paris, opened a shadow theatre in London, at the Great Room in Panton Street, the effects of which seem to have resembled those of the Eidophusikon, which it preceded by about six years, rather than those of the shadow play proper. It was scenic rather than dramatic, the principal piece consisting of a shipwreck accompanied by thunder and lightning. Another striking piece was entitled *The Metamorphosis of a Magician* and showed the shape of an elephant dissolving, like Philipsthal's Dr. Franklin in the Phantasmagoria, into a skeleton. The price of admission to Ambroise's Ombres Chinoises was five shillings, but the back seats were reduced to half a crown when the Christmas season was over.

In the following year two rival showmen, Braville and Menucci, set up, first at the Great Room, St. Albans Street, Pall Mall, and then at the Temple of Apollo, but they met with little success. Ambroise took his shadows on tour to the provinces for a time in 1778 when the Great Room, Panton Street, was occupied by Italian shadow showmen. In the same year Philip Astley, founder of Astley's, who had already shown an interest in the shadow theatre, included Chinese shades in an entertainment of conjuring and horsemanship at 22 Piccadilly. Shadow shows continued to feature in Astley's repertoire for the next ten years. Shades were also exhibited at Sadler's Wells and at the Chinese Academy in Tooley Street, where the screen was 14 ft. long, giving ample scope for effective processions.

The items in all these shows were very much alike. They all included the most popular theme of all, *The Broken Bridge*. The basic form of this rudimentary spectacle is as follows:

The two arms of the bridge arch over a stream, but do not meet. A party of ducks crosses leisurely from one bank to the other. Then a labourer appears on the right-hand side of the bridge and begins to swing a pick-axe to loosen the stones at the end, and these fragments of masonry are seen to fall into the water. The labourer sings as he works and in France his song is always 'Sur le pont d'Avignon'. A traveller now comes from the opposite side and hails the

Two scenes from the shadow play *Kazandonis* performed in Athens in 1962, set in the times of the Greek struggle for independence. *Above:* The hero Kazandonis kneels by his wife who has fainted while a Turkish mercenary prepares to attack him. *Below:* Aly Pasha with a 'good' Greek (*right*) and a 'bad' Greek outside his palace labourer, who, being hard of hearing, is long in replying. The traveller explains that he is anxious to cross and wishes to know how he can do this. The labourer picks away and sings: 'The ducks and geese, they all swim over.' The irritated traveller then asks how wide the stream is and the labourer sings: 'When you're in the middle you're half-way over.' The traveller then inquires how deep the water may be and receives the exasperating answer that if he will only throw in a stone he will find the bottom soon enough. At this point a boatman comes into view rowing a little skiff, his backbone pivoted so that his body can move to and fro. The traveller bargains with him and is at last taken across the water after many misadventures, one of them with a crocodile which opens its jaws and threatens to swallow the boat. Meanwhile the ill-natured labourer advances too far on his side of the broken bridge and falls into the stream, together with an immense block of stone, to be instantly devoured by the crocodile. When the turmoil has subsided the placid ducks swim once more across the water and the curtain falls.

This piece probably originated in France and was part of the repertoire of Nicolas Médard Audinot, a former actor, who gave a series of shadow shows in 1760 at the Théâtre des Italiens, chiefly with figures based on the Harlequinade, and then set up a little shadow theatre at the Foire St. Germain.

A decade later *Le Pont Cassé* was the principal piece shown by François Dominique Seraphin, a young man of twenty-three who, after travelling in Italy and Germany, opened a shadow show at Versailles. The novelty and ingenuity of his figures and performances attracted such large audiences that Seraphin was soon able to establish permanent and more commodious premises in the Palais Royale. His first performance there was given on September 8th, 1784, and from then on Seraphin gave two shows on every Sunday and feast day, and one on every weekday. The price of admission was twenty-four sous. Special music for the entertainment was composed and played on the harpsichord by Theodore Mozin. In addition to *Le Pont Cassé* the repertoire included *Arlequin Corsaire*, *Le Magician Rothomago*, *La Chasse aux Canards* (a great favourite), *L'Embarras du Ménage*, *The Enchanted Forest*, and circus acts with animals, dancers, clowns, and tightrope walkers. During the Revolution Seraphin cleverly adapted his shadow show to the spirit of the time, making *Le Pont Cassé* represent the Republican point of view, and in order to compete with the new panorama entertainment he varied his programme with staggering fire effects.

After his death in 1800 his enterprise was carried on until 1844 by his nephew, who enlarged the scope of the show by adding transformation scenes, or what he called *Metamorphoses*. A sheet of shadow figures intended for a toy shadow theatre, published by the celebrated firm of Péllérin at Épinal in Alsace and entitled *Metamorphoses*, gives a good idea of these transformation scenes. The figures, when pasted on stout cardboard and cut out, can be operated by means of a piece of thread and made to undergo complete changes before the eyes of the audience, becoming quite different characters or taking on the shape of some grotesque beast or curious object. After the death of Seraphin's nephew his son-in-law took over the theatre and transferred it from the Palais Royale to the boulevard Montmartre. He combined the shadow show with effects closely allied to those of the Phantasmagoria and with what he called a 'Diaphanorama'.

Seraphin's shadow theatre closed on August 15th, 1879, brought to an end by the Siege of Paris. By this time it had to a certain extent lost its purely popular character. The theatres of both Seraphin in Paris and of Ambroise and Astley in London, while preserving the popular appeal of the shades, had also addressed the fashionable world. As the nineteenth century progressed, the shadows tended to become more and more an entertainment for sophisticated society and the concern of artists and writers, and this despite the fact that the traditional fairy-tale and humorous subjects were kept alive by the toy shadow theatres of the period and by provincial shows such as that of Père Eudel at Crotoy.

As early as 1778 Goethe had become interested in the shadow show, and introduced a charming shadow interlude in his masque *Das Jahrmarktsfest zu Plundersweilen*. The scene is an annual fair in a small provincial town. A shadow showman wanders across the ground playing a little concertina and crying, 'Orgelum, orgelei, Dudeldumdei', as he sets up his screen and arranges his puppets. His theme is grandiose: he shows the Creation, the Fall, and the history of Man up to the time of the Flood. The curtain rises on a totally dark screen which is very slowly illuminated as God says, 'Let there be light'; then the silhouettes of sun, moon, stars, a tree, and an animal pass before the spectators, to be followed by Adam, Eve, the Serpent, and the Expulsion.

71

Next, knights and ladies are shown dallying 'in the green shade'. 'Men are rapidly multiplying and are very sinful,' says the showman. 'How can the Lord God put up with behaviour such as this?' The Flood engulfs the amorous couples and Mercury (an allusion to a literary periodical) flies down to speak the final words, 'Thanks be to God.' This little play was actually performed on one occasion with figures cut out by Einsiedel.

It was natural that the German romantics, with their deep interest in folklore and popular art, should be drawn to the shadow theatre. Performances were given regularly in Berlin during the 1820's, and Brentano, Achim von Arnim, Tieck, and Uhland all wrote scripts—sophisticated, fantastic, symbolic themes which yet would not have seemed entirely alien to the audiences who had laughed at Karagöz and trembled when Sita was committed to the flames.

In France, some ten years after Seraphin's theatre had closed down, in 1881, Rudolphe Salis started a cabaret called Le Chat Noir after Poe's Black Tom Cat. It was in Montmartre on the boulevard de Rochechouart, in a studio which Salis had fitted up in a disused post office. Later he moved to a new locale in the rue Victor Masse. Salis was an extraordinary character who had tried a dozen professions before finding his true bent as a showman. He had been an unsuccessful mathematician, a caricaturist, an engraver, an archaeologist, and a painter. The cabaret proved to be the perfect medium for his exhibitionism and his flair for publicity. He once announced his own death in the weekly paper issued by Le Chat Noir, wrote his own obituary, put up a notice on the door saying 'Open because of Death', and then attended his own funeral in a costume of cloth of gold. He also had a rare gift for detecting and exploiting talent. Le Chat Noir became a meeting-place for painters, poets, and musicians whom Salis persuaded to entertain his clientele in various ways. Among them were Alphonse Allais, Emile Goudeau, Verlaine, Lautrec, Maurice Rollinat, François Coppée, Forain, Willette, Paul Alexis, Jules Jouy, Maurice Donnay, and, at one time, Sarah Bernhardt.

The cabaret was elaborately decorated in period style with armour, rusty swords, tapestries, antlers, wrought iron, lanterns, wood-carvings in the medieval style, Gothic windows, a great open hearth, and a huge picture by Willette showing a crowd of pierrots, art students, singers, and girls, with a death's head grinning from the clouds behind them. This was the 'great hall' open to all. Behind it was a smaller room, called the Institut, reserved for artists and heavy drinkers, where the waiters were dressed in the green uniform worn by members of the French Academy. Here weekly literary discussions were held and every evening there was a reading of new poetry or a song recital. As one of these nightly entertainments, Georges Auriol and Henry Somm had set up a little puppet theatre. During a performance on the spur of the moment Henri Rivière stretched a serviette across the proscenium and threw on to it the shadows of some *serjents de ville* he had hastily cut out of cardboard. This was the haphazard beginning of the Théâtre des Ombres du Chat Noir.

The shades were at first cut out of cardboard, but were later made of zinc and were about 12 in. high. They were not articulated, but relied on clever cutting and witty comment. A fixed screen was built, measuring about 4 by 3 ft., and gradually elaborate machinery was introduced to operate intricate lighting changes and fabulous scenic effects. The mode of operation was this: the figures and the principle furnishings were pressed against the screen and the tableau was passed across it while effects of cloud, light, or water painted on sheets of glass were held in grooves top and bottom. There were at least thirty grooves for the glass sheets to slide in and they needed ten or twelve men to shift them. The figures and effects nearest the screen were always dead black, the secondary silhouettes were in a grey tint, and distant effects were still lighter. The glass sheets were illuminated by a powerful oxy-hydrogen lamp burning with a naked flame at a distance of about 10 ft. from the screen.

In his memoirs of Le Chat Noir, Paul Jeanne says that the shadow show always opened with a very simple piece by Henry Somm, called *L'Éléphant*. A negro crossed the screen tugging at a rope. For a long time nothing was seen but the shadow of the taut rope. Then a knot appeared, travelled slowly across the screen, and vanished. At long last an elephant moved ponderously into view at the end of the rope. He stopped and solemnly deposited a large turd out of which sprang a beautiful rose.

The main pieces of the programme fell into two groups: those which were accompanied by an impromptu commentary, usually brilliantly delivered by Salis, and those which were combined with a specially written script, nearly always in verse and very often sung. There were, in addition, some pieces in which song and speech were hardly used at all except for some sharp exclamation or word of command. Such was Caran d'Ache's epic evocation of the Napoleonic army *L'Épopée*. He made a speciality of long lines and masses of troops, not all on the same plane, but presented in perspective. He brought before his Parisian audiences company after company of the Old Guard and troop after troop of cuirassiers, grenadiers, lancers, artillery, and cavalry, the profiles diminishing in height as the figures receded from the eye. Caran d'Ache achieved astonishing effects of solidity, immensity, and space and succeeded in creating the impression of a vast mass of men under arms marching resolutely forward to victory or death.

This realistic art, far removed from the shadow play of the Orient, at once recalls, both in treatment and subject-matter, the panoramas of Colonel Langlois. And it approached even more closely to the Panorama and the Diorama when Henri Rivière, the originator of Le Chat Noir shadow shows, added colour to Caran d'Ache's perspective. He cut out some parts of the figures and objects, leaving a thin outline, rather in the manner of the Chinese and Japanese puppets, which, as a passionate student of Japanese art, he may well have known; and into the openings thus made he inserted slips of tinted paper through which the light would shine to produce a glow of colour. And for the naphtha lamp or gas jet Rivière substituted a magic lantern with painted slides to provide the black silhouettes with a coloured background. Then he went further and employed two magic lanterns which enabled him to dissolve one landscape background into another as the figures moved. Henri Rivière was a poet and some of the pieces he designed are reported by a reliable witness, Louis Morin, who himself collaborated in the productions of Le Chat Noir, to have evoked a fleeting fairy-tale world, a dream that vanished before the ravished eye had plumbed the mystery of its gossamer fragility. Yet the lithographic reproductions of some of the scenes and incidental details, published by Vernot, have very little poetry; they are mechanical and prosaic when set beside the freely designed figures and properties of the Karagöz plays, and seldom show a trace of the robust fantasy, exaggeration, and humour of the traditional shadow theatre. Everything seems to have depended on the gusto of the performance. Albert Tinchant's brilliant interpretation of Georges Fragerolle's sentimental song 'Clair de Lune' transported Le Chat Noir audiences. The last words of the dying soldier:

Le Sacre de Clémenceau

'Je rève a ma mie aux si doux appas
A ma mère aussi qui m'attend là-bas
A mon vieux clocher qui chante a la brune
Au clair de la lune'

and the words of the storm-tossed sailor:

'Je pense a la Vierge aimante aux doux yeux
A l'étoile d'or qui sourit aux cieux
Au Christ implorant pour nous sur la dune
Au clair de la lune'

were accompanied by a series of romantic moonlit scenes by Rivière, dissolving one into another—a forest, a lake, the glittering ocean, a winter landscape flinging back the glow of an orange-hued rising moon, a churchyard deep in snow, all of which enchanted an audience who had never seen a colour film. Both the poem and the shades, as we shall see, are very close in feeling and imagery to the magic-lantern shows popular in England a few years later in far less sophisticated circles.

Rivière's greatest success, *La Marche à l'Étoile*, was a pure spectacle the effect of which must have been out of all proportion to Fragerolle's trite verse. It featured a great procession of worshippers journeying to Bethlehem guided by the star—shepherds, soldiers, lepers, slaves with their fetters loosened, beggars, fishermen, and kings. And at the end Golgotha flamed forth blood-red. Rivière was quick to recognize the themes best suited to his moving-picture medium, and besides *La Marche à l'Étoile* he produced *The Wandering Jew*, *The Prodigal Son*, in which some of the figures were cleverly articulated, and *The Temptation of St. Anthony*, all of which demanded grandiose scenes and a vast number of figures.

A particularly impressive show which combined all Caran d'Ache's tricks of perspective and Rivière's use of poetic coloured backgrounds was *Le Sphinx*, with shades by Vignola accompanied by a stately chant by Fragerolle. Centuries pass, peoples come and go; Egyptians, Assyrians, Jews, Persians, Greeks, Romans, Arabs, the Crusaders, Napoleon, and finally British soldiers of the

Noah's Ark and The Retreat from Moscow, c. 1820 (both from the Barnes Collection)

Pull Devil, Pull Baker, c. 1840 (Science Museum, London)

Three early hand-painted panoramic slides

C. GOODWIN NORTON

Is a most experienced Exhibitor, and Author of the Text Book on the subject:

"The Lantern, and how to use it."

Everything necessary is provided, and the whole apparatus can be set up without interfering with the furniture or fixtures.

The illuminant is the Oxyhydrogen Limelight, which is inodorous and safe, no fluid of any kind being employed.

This Entertainment can be given alone, or in conjunction with C. Goodwin Norton's well-known Animated Photographs.

SPECIMEN PROGRAMME.

OVERTURE.

CURTAIN.

A Country Cottage by day—Evening (moonlight night) —Winter comes with falling snow.

The various changes are made imperceptibly, giving a most natural effect.

"MYSTIFY & Co."

An original fairy tale, illustrated by beautiful hand-painted pictures with rapid changes and illusions.

THE HOUSES OF PARLIAMENT,

with moon appearing and ripples on the water.

THE EIFFEL TOWER,

with revolving light and illumination.

THE HOTEL DE VILLE, PARIS,

with charming effect by lighting up each window.

"THE PIED PIPER OF HAMELIN."

This well-known Poem has been shortened and illustrated by a very clever Artist.

FLOWER STUDIES,

illustrating the new process of Photography in Colours.
The flowers are shewn on the screen as a photograph and then gradually become coloured. The most successful are a Rose, Vase of Hollyhocks and a Tiger Lilly.

Animal Studies at the Zoo.

RECITATION   "How Bill Adams Won the Battle of Waterloo." (illustrated most humorously).

READING   ...   "Dora"   ...   *Tennyson.*

"The Soldier's Dream on the Battle Field."

STORIES FOR CHILDREN.

The House that Jack Built.   **Fairy Tales.**

Various Comic and Amusing Pictures all free from any objectional feature.

The Wonderful Choreutoscope or Mechanical Dancer.

Portraits of the Royal Family and Eminent Persons.

𝕲𝖔𝖉 𝕾𝖆𝖛𝖊 𝖙𝖍𝖊 𝕶𝖎𝖓𝖌.

GOOD-NIGHT.

nineties file past the great recumbent figure of the Sphinx, who is left at last alone, a cold, misty, grey form floating in the desolation of a blue-green Nile twilight.

The great success enjoyed by Le Chat Noir had encouraged other cabarets to make the shadow show part of the entertainment they offered. Among these was the Lyon d'Or, opened by F. Trombert in 1892. The shadow theatre was known as Le Théâtre des Ombres Lyriques and the repertoire consisted only of trifling lyrical pieces, sung or recited. The performance was distinguished less by its programme than by the technique Trombert employed. Instead of the naphtha lamp and the magic lanterns which Rivière had used, he introduced oxy-acetylene lamps and condensers to project his images, thus approaching more closely to the cinema technique. The subtitle of the show, Théâtre des Projections Lumineuse, was precisely accurate.

After 1897, when Rudolphe Salis died and Le Chat Noir closed down, many other *théâtres d'ombres* sprang up in Paris. Among these were the Boîte à Musique; the Conservatoire Montmartre, where Alfred de Musset's *Ballade à la Lune* was made into a shadow play; Le Théâtre Antoine, where Rivière's *Wandering Jew* was performed; Le Théâtre des Mathurins, where Lucien Metivet wrote the poems and cut the shadows for two entertaining pieces, *La Belle au Bois Dormant* and *Aladin*; and Les Quatz'arts, which most nearly resembled Le Chat Noir in character, reviving the most successful of Henri Rivière's shadow shows, including *La March à L'Étoile* and *L'Enfant Prodigue*, and enlarging the repertoire after the turn of the century with several new pieces, among them Steinlein's *Une Page d'Amour*, *La Marche des Députés* by Dominique Bonnaud and Numa Blès, and an aquatic fantasy by Edmond Lempereur called *Le Serpent du Mer* and *La Chevauchée des Satryes* with verse by Gaston Pollonais and shades by Brunner.

In 1904 Dominique Bonnaud and Numa Blès opened a new shadow theatre known as La Lune Rousse, which survived until the outbreak of the First World War in 1914. Here also something of the atmosphere of Le Chat Noir was revived, and among many new pieces *Le Sacre de Clémenceau* by Bonnaud, with shadows by Lempereur, seems to have been particularly lively. Lempereur made more emphatic use of Rivière's technique of cutting away part of the figures. The faces and flesh parts of his shades, and sometimes parts of the clothing, were cut away, leaving them brilliantly white, so that these

Above left: C. Goodwin Norton with his triple lantern. (Science Museum, London)
Above right: French nineteenth-century magic lantern of japanned tin with decorative press markings. (Barnes Collection)
Below: Programme of a lantern entertainment given by C. Goodwin Norton. (Science Museum, London)

vigorously drawn figures looked like animated pen-and-ink sketches rather than silhouettes. They were known as *les ombres blanches*.

This silhouette art of the fashionable world was paralleled by street entertainments for the poor given by wandering showmen, like the one in Goethe's masque. These humble little shadow plays were much closer in spirit to the slapstick Karagöz shows than to the Montmartre spectacles, and their memory has been uniquely preserved in Mayhew's report of his interview in 1853 with a typical exhibitor of the Chinese shades in the streets of London. In this absorbing and most moving study the old showman speaks to us directly:

'The proper name of my exhibition', he says, 'is Lez Hombres or the Shades; that's the proper name for it, for Baron Rothschild told me when I performed before him. We calls it the Chinese show.' He goes on to tell us that the *ombres chinoises* had been seen on the streets for about twenty-six years, and he names three men who travelled, like himself, with their shadows: Thomas Paris, who 'was the first man that brought out the *ombres* in the street', 'a short stout man, very old', Jim Macklin, and Paul Herring.

Macklin and Herring were both actors who probably went round with the shades when they had no work in the theatre. 'Paul Herring did excellent well with it, nothing less than thirty shillings or two pounds a night. He didn't stop long at it. . . . He only done it for a lark. He was hard up for money and got it.' Herring, whose real name was Bill Smith, played the part of Diolinski in *Mazeppa* at Astley's in 1831 and later became a famous pantomime clown. One of the most popular of the street shadow plays, *Cobbler Jobson*, has been attributed to him, but Mayhew's showman, who never tells us his name, says he was the author of this piece, as well as of *Kitty Biling the Pot* or *The Woodchopper's Frolic* and *Billy Button's Journey to Brentwood on Horseback and his favourite Servant Jeremiah Stitchem in want of a Situation*, the last adapted from an equestrian turn first brought out at Astley's. The showman probably means that he adapted his pieces from well-known sources. *Kitty Biling the Pot* has much in common with Seraphin's *Le Chat Voleur*, and later on in his interview with Mayhew the showman admits that he took this theme from Paris.

The Broken Bridge was inevitably part of his repertoire. 'I don't know who composed that,' he declares. 'It's too far gone by to trace who the first author is, but it was adapted from the piece brought out formerly at Drury Lane Theatre. Old ancient gentlemen has told me so who saw it, when it was first brought out, and they're old enough to be my grandfather. I've new revised it.'

These travelling showmen generally worked with a Punch and Judy frame with a piece of calico stretched in front of it and three candles behind. During the day they would perform the Punch and Judy puppet show and at night they would exhibit the shadows, usually after seven o'clock. The best pitch of all was Regent Street, but Leicester Square was a very good place and so was Islington. The showmen were in the habit of going out in couples. The one interviewed by Mayhew spoke the various parts in different voices, standing in front and playing the pandanean pipe ('That's the real word for the pipe, from the Romans, when they first invaded England'). His partner manipulated the figures, which appear to have been jointed in much the same way as the Turkish shades.

The exhibition began with a sailor dancing a hornpipe; next, a tightrope dancer appeared; and after that there was hornpipe dancing, and then the main piece of the evening began, either one of those already mentioned or *Billy Waters* or *Bull-Baiting*. Mayhew's showman thought *Kitty Biling the Pot* 'one of the most beautifullest scenes in the world' and once tried to take Ramsgate Theatre to act it with human figures on a large screen, but the rent was two pounds a night and that was too much for him. He describes this play, as well as *Cobbler Jobson*, in full detail, and after reading his graphic account we seem to have stood in Leicester Square with the crowd, entranced by the shadows moving across the tiny screen, carried away by the marvellous effect of the fire, with sparks flying up the chimney when Kitty blows it up with a pair of enormous bellows, amazed by the skill with which her mother is made to squint up the chimney with one eye while with the other she looks into the pot, and delighted with the boisterous ending when the woodchopper, coming in from his work, asks, '"Where's my supper?" "Oh, a nasty big he-she-tom cat has been and stolen the mutton out of the pot." "What?" passionate directly, you see. Then she says, "You must put up with bread-and-cheese." He answers, "That don't suit some people," and then comes a fight. The Spring-heeled Jack is introduced and he carries off the fireplace and pot and all. *Exeunt*. That's the end of the piece and a very good one it was.'

The showman reveals that on an average he took five shillings a night, but when during the Christmas season he attended parties he generally made a pound. 'If you goes to a gentleman's house, it's according to whether you behave yourself in a superior sort of manner, but if you have any vulgarity about you, you must exaunt, and that's no recommendation.' He complains bitterly of the boys and young children who disturb his show of an evening, following him about, pushing their way to the front of the audience, even throwing stones, spoiling the pleasure of the serious adult viewers, for whom the show is intended, with their noise and never themselves contributing more than a farthing or a halfpenny to the collection and that very rarely. 'No, girls ain't better behaved than boys; they was much wus. I'd sooner have fifty boys round me than four girls. The impertinence of them is above bearing. They come carrying babies and pushing and crowding and tearing one another to pieces. "You're afore me — I was fust — No, you wasn't — Yes, I was!"—and that's the way they go on.'

It was sometimes a dangerous business manipulating the shadows by candle-light, especially when the crowd was disorderly. Once when Mayhew's show-man was performing at Islington Green some drunken people knocked over the whole show and it went up in flames with his mate inside.

Travelling showmen vanished from the London streets early in the present century. And although, by combining her exquisite silhouettes with the film technique, Lotte Reiniger has revived the art of the shadow play as a shadow film, the entertainment of the *ombres chinoises* as it was known in Europe before the First World War has ceased to exist. The affinity between the Chinese shades and the cinema that ousted them was acknowledged in a German film called *Warning Shadows* in which a story is told by a wandering showman with a little portable shadow show. He comes as a welcome entertainer to a house in which a distressing emotional situation has been disclosed by the shadows of human actors flung on to the drawn blinds. The showman's little silhouettes project the shadows of the fate awaiting each of the human beings if they cannot overcome their desires.

6

Dissolving Views

That which was now a horse, even with a thought
The rack dislimns and makes as indistinct
As water is in water.

HAZLITT

FROM the time of its invention in the seventeenth century the magic lantern, as we have seen, was often introduced as an aid to the more elaborate effects of the many forms of moving pictures which provided popular entertainment during the centuries preceding our own. Even the shadow play could not dispense with the lantern in the later stages of its development in Paris. As for the magic-lantern show itself, it became a major amusement, both public and private, throughout the Victorian period. And whereas the impact made by the dioramas, panoramas, and shadow shows of that time can be experienced only at second hand through the accounts of eyewitnesses and a few surviving fragments, the celebrated effects achieved by the lantern can still be enjoyed, for the manufacture of lanterns and slides became so extensive an industry that the most amateur collector finds no difficulty in acquiring substantial remains of it.

During the early years of the nineteenth century the cry of itinerant magic-lantern showmen, many of them Italian, was among the commonest sounds in the streets of the larger cities of Europe during the winter months. The name given to their entertainment in England, the Galantee show, derived from the foreigner's cry of 'Galante so, galante so', 'so' being his pronunciation of the English 'show', 'galante' his word for 'fine'. The showmen generally carried a hand organ as well as their magic box and travelled in couples, one man playing the organ, the other exhibiting the transparencies. They usually performed in private houses into which they were invited in answer to their call. A writer in *The Penny Magazine* for 1845 remembered having seen many such performances in London during his youth and describes the slides as 'for the most part exceedingly grotesque'.

Two contemporary records of English galantee showmen yield a glimpse of the kinds of subjects which were applauded during the first half of the century and also conjure up vivid images of the lanternists themselves.

William Hone writes in 1828 of a Twelfth Night ten years earlier when he answered the nocturnal cry of 'Galantee show' by asking the man into his house where a children's party was in progress. He was astonished to find that the subjects were all religious. One set of slides showed the Prodigal Son carousing with his boon companions at the Swan Inn, Stratford, where the landlady at the bar scored double for every fresh order; another sequence represented Noah's Ark, and a third, entitled *Pull Devil, Pull Baker*, portrayed the last judgement upon a baker who sold bread short of weight and was eventually carried off to hell in his own basket.

Hone's interest was keenly aroused, for he recognized all three sets of slides as versions of miracle plays performed in England five centuries earlier. He recalled that Autolycus in *A Winter's Tale* 'compos'd a motion of the Prodigal Son' for exhibition at wakes, fairs, and bear-baitings; and he recognized this magic-lantern show as a continuation of that tradition. This is all the more fascinating when the show is viewed in perspective as part of the development of the moving picture, for it reveals the persistence of the supernatural themes associated with the projection of images not only in Kircher's day but in remote antiquity. Hone's showman gave an extremely lively commentary on each scene, while his assistant in the next room played country dance and other tunes on the street organ during the entire performance. They told Hone that their show had been exactly the same for many years and that they had no other slides than the three sets.

The type of slide Hone saw—a long, narrow glass containing a series of images which, passed slowly in front of the lens, gave a sense of movement—was still being produced well after the middle of the last century. Numbers of examples survive in public and private collections and are not infrequently to be found on the market stall or in the sale-room. There is a slide of *Pull Devil, Pull Baker* on exhibition in the Science Museum, South Kensington, which precisely corresponds to Hone's description of the transparency he saw. The figures are painted on clear glass and brightly coloured red and blue except for the Devil, who appears as a black silhouette with cloven hooves, horns, and an immensely long tail. Two similar slides in the Barnes Collection show Death seizing a miser and a *Noah's Ark*, a particularly fine panoramic glass, possibly of French origin. These two slides measure about 17 by 4 in. and are very freely drawn and coloured in delicious greens, yellows, and browns, the images in the *Noah's Ark* of ostriches, peacocks, daintily stepping long-necked deer, camels, elephants with curling trunks, prancing horses, Noah in biblical costume, and Mrs. Noah looking like Queen Anne, much resembling pottery decoration and pottery figures of the late eighteenth and early nineteenth centuries.

A remarkable collection of long slides of more primitive character than these, and with the images shown on a black background instead of on the clear glass, is in the possession of Mr. Hermann Hecht. Despite their apparent antiquity, they are probably not much more than one hundred and fifty years old and were probably made in central Europe, for they have obvious affinities with the religious glass pictures of the anonymous folk artists of Bohemia, Moravia, south Germany, and Austria, dating from that time. They are all the work of the same artist, for not only are the facial types consistent but the identical simple but effective shorthand is used throughout in the rendering of anatomy. It is likely that the compositions are based on engravings: they are essentially linear and indeed, like the glass pictures, are closely related to the popular prints sold at central European fairs at the end of the eighteenth century. The drawing is strong and rhythmical, with the heads exaggerated; the brilliant colours—red, intense blue, warm brown, and dark green—are used in a purely descriptive fashion, as in Gothic stained glass. And these powerful figures, when cast life-size upon the screen, unconsciously achieve what the most scholarly efforts of the Gothic Revivalists failed to do: they recapture the full, robust flavour of medieval art. They delight us, as medieval imagery delights us, with the marvellous unity of vision they express.

The personages of the Scriptures, Christ and the Saints, are presented as grand symbolic figures, and yet they are so much part of everyday life that they can be treated with the utmost familiarity and on occasion with ribald humour. The whale, whose giant head fills a corner of the slide portraying Jonah, smirks and rolls his eye knowingly after having vomited his tenant upon the dry land; the vigorous lions whose attitudes are repeated on the pottery, pastry moulds, and village carvings of the period fall with smiling relish on the men who had wrongly accused Daniel, more vivid even than the graphic account of them in the Bible: 'The lions had their mastery of them and brake all their bones in pieces or ever they came to the bottom of the den.' In the scene of the conversion of St. Paul it is not the saint but the effect of the blinding light on the mule which has stirred the artist. The terrified animal kicks his heels with full force towards the spectator, charging the unnatural glare.

With the projected figure of Christ on the Cross this anonymous art rises to a level beyond the sphere of entertainment. This calm, jet-bearded, muscular form, a commanding symbol of strength rather than suffering, brilliantly luminous against its stark black background, seems more alive than the breathing audience and impresses itself on the memory and imagination as only a pictorial masterpiece can do.

The spirit which animates these slides was still present in those which Hone saw; and it was alive, too, in the showman, a man of the people. We know this because when Hone—who, despite the interest he felt, had, like all modern men, lost the unity of vision enjoyed by the makers of the slides—was shocked by the familiarity and humour with which the religious themes were treated, and remonstrated with the lanternist, it was impossible to make him comprehend that there might be objections to such an entertainment. When he left the house he gave Hone a card inscribed: 'The Royal Gallantee Show, provided by Jos. Leverage, 7 Ely Court, Holborn Hill', and with a thrill of excitement his host remembered that this was the very spot where the last performance in England took place of the mystery entitled *The Play of Christ's Passion*.

Some thirty years after Hone's encounter with Mr. Leverage, Mayhew interviewed a gallantee showman, one of the last of his kind, 'a short, thick-set man with small puckered-up eyes and dressed in an old brown velveteen shooting jacket', who began his story with, 'I was fifty-five last New Year's Day.' He was brought up first in a workhouse, then with his grandfather, a tailor, and was apprenticed to a sweep who treated him cruelly and fed him

A scene from *Uncle Tom's Cabin*
(Barnes Collection)

A scene in the Arctic by Carpenter and Westley
(Science Museum, London)

Two mid-nineteenth-century hand-painted slides

Lever or rocking slide. Part of the picture is painted on a glass fixed in the frame while the ship is delineated on a cover glass held by the brass ring so that it can be tilted by the lever at the side, thus giving the effect of tossing on the sea

Rosalie at the gate, from *A Peep Behind the Scenes*, with painted background

Kitchen scene from *A Muslin Frock*

Late Victorian hand-coloured photographic slides made from life models to illustrate moral tales and popular songs and poems

Interior from *There Is No Rose*

Interior from *Probable Sons*. The long exposure was made in the open air without the aid of lights; the 'ceiling' of the room is the sky

poorly. After seven 'sorrowful years' he left the sweep, bought pandean pipes, and became the mate of an organ-grinder. Next he threw in his lot with an Italian and a dancing bear, and after trouble with the police joined a showman who exhibited clockwork figures. During the coldest winter months the figures were put by and the two men went round with a magic lantern. They showed their slides on a white sheet or on the ceiling 'in the houses of the gentlefolk, and the schools where there was a breaking up. It was shown by way of a treat to the scholars. . . . We had ten-and-sixpence and fifteen shillings for each performance and did very well indeed.'

The subjects shown were quite different from those seen by Hone and in some respects approached those exhibited by the street shadow showmen, for they included a *Harlequinade* and *Billy Button*. Long slides of the *Harlequinade* are still found, but no slides showing characters from *Billy Button* have survived. It is possible that these may have been silhouette slides directly taken from the shadow show of the same name.

The showman goes on to say: 'Green's dead and all the line's dead but me. The galantee show don't answer because magic lanterns are so cheap in the shops. When we started magic lanterns wasn't so common; but we can't keep hold of a good thing in these times. It was a reg'lar thing for Christmas—the galantee show.'

The slides shown by the itinerant lanternists were probably all of the panoramic kind, long strips of glass measuring anything from 14 to 20 in. Apart from the examples already described, many finely painted transparencies were produced prior to about 1840. There are two slides in the Barnes Collection showing Napoleon in retreat from Moscow which have the precision and vitality of West's sheets of characters for the Juvenile Drama, and it seems probable that many of the artists who worked for the Toy Theatre may also have painted slides. These Napoleonic subjects show the Emperor on horseback wheeling about with upraised sword to attack a Cossack leaping upon him in the act of firing. Fierce Cossack riders pursue the French cavalry, a wounded horse struggles in the snow by an upturned cart, and an icicle-hung tree stands grimly against the black background.

Another long slide in the same collection and of about the same date, 1820, shows the havoc wrought by a mad bull. A horse drawing a cart, with an old man and woman sitting in the back, runs away; a man and a boy are seen pelting down the road in a fright; a donkey on which a young woman is riding begins to buck, nostrils distended, eye rolling; and then after them all comes the heavy, mottled bull with lowered head, followed by the panting farmer in striped stockings waving his stick, quite unable to catch up with the frenzied beast. Each figure or group of figures is isolated on the black ground.

Slides similar to these were still being shown at the end of the century: the firm of Poulton and Son were advertising comic panoramic slides as late as 1895. The convention of the brightly coloured figures on a black ground remained unaltered, but the drawing was less firm, the types became increasingly more grotesque. It is curious that the figures on these slides often preserve the costume of the 1820's, even when some other detail, such as the introduction in the sequence of a helmeted policeman, proves that the glass must have been painted considerably later.

Panoramic slides counterfeit movement in a very primitive way, but the desire to animate the projected image soon led to the invention of many ingenious mechanical slides, all of which were being made before 1858, the date of a treatise on slides published by Winsor and Newton and written by Edward Groom. He states that such slides were being shown at that time only in public institutions and were not used for private entertainment, so they could not have been so widely distributed as they were towards the close of the nineteenth century.

The commonest kind of mechanical slide, and probably the first to be invented, was the slipping slide. It consists of a framed piece of glass with one or two supplementary movable pieces which can be pulled out to one or both sides or passed one across another. Sometimes the pictures are painted in their entirety, including all positions of the figure or object, on the framed glass, while the shifting pieces are covered with lampblack to shut out the parts which must be excluded. The action of a boy astride a donkey, the animal kicking with its hind legs and the boy beating it, can be produced in this way; the chequered limbs of a harlequin can be made to fly asunder, and an old woman will lose her wig and bonnet in a gale. In other instances, painting occurs on all the glasses, that on the slips being brushed on to the clear glass. The gigantic, formidable head of a monkey will appear on the screen and suddenly its great red eyes will begin to move grotesquely from side to side while its jaws open and shut; a rubicund monk will roll his eyes and smack his thick lips at the sight of a tankard of ale; Queen Victoria will be disclosed one moment in court dress, the next in widow's weeds.

Among the vast number of slipping-slide subjects which survive there is one in Mr. Hermann Hecht's collection of Prince Charles in the oak tree which provides a charming contrast to the coarser themes more often preferred. The oak, with foliage rendered in a light, elegant manner reminiscent of Gainsborough, fills the centre of the slide. The Prince perches among the leaves and Cromwell's men pass under the tree as the shifting glass is moved to the side. A similar slide shows a review of the Fleet, with ships crossing a wide, romantic bay; and yet another simulates the movement of a train over a viaduct. Viewers seldom notice that the wheels are not actually revolving.

Another simple device for producing a moving image was the lever slide. It combines two glasses, one of which, enclosed in a brass ring attached to a lever, is worked up and down over the other. The most familiar example portrays a ship tossing on the ocean in storm or sunshine. The sea and sky are painted on one slide and on the other, the one that moves, appears the ship. Other effective lever slides show a horse drinking or a man hammering, while one of the commonest and most enchanting images achieved in this way is of a seesaw with a boy at one end and a girl at the other. An impression similar to that produced by the lever is sometimes contrived by means of an eccentric movement; thus a ship can be made to dance up and down by turning a handle constantly in one direction.

More convincing, more striking, than any of these are the animated scenes thrown upon the screen by the rack-work slide. Here the glasses are mounted on the same principle as in the lever slide, but the motion results from the action of rack and pinion, one of the glasses being set in a cogged frame. Magical semblances of rotation are created by the rack-work slide: with its aid the lanternist can project a picture of the planets revolving about the sun, can set the sails of a windmill turning, can make a wheel go round. A slide in the Barnes Collection shows a mill-wheel in action with the mill stream falling in a foaming cascade, brilliantly white against the dark intensity of the minutely detailed thicket surrounding it. This is an unusually poetic version of a favourite subject; and there is something extraordinarily exciting to viewers accustomed only to the moving photographic image in the spectacle of this finely executed romantic painting in motion.

The rack-work slide produces a conspicuously smooth, continuous movement such as that of smoke rising from a chimney, or of flames issuing from a volcano or burning building, and it is upon this form of glass that the well-known comic representation is based of a man swallowing rats. The screen is completely filled with the close-up of a bearded man in a nightcap asleep in bed. The figure is at least twice as large as life and coloured in bright Toy Theatre crimsons and blues. The sleeper's wide mouth opens and shuts with every snore, and into that gaping cavern runs a succession of long-tailed rats climbing one by one over the sprigged and billowy eiderdown. The horrific impact of this slide on a child who had never seen a film is graphically conveyed by Eleanor Farjeon in *A Nursery of the Nineties*.

Pulley slides, finally, consist of two discs of glass mounted in brass rings and turned in contrary directions by means of two bands, one of which is crossed, running in a groove round the periphery of each ring and passing to a hand-operated wheel. This kind of frame was used for the very popular so-called chromatrope effects, many of the glasses for which survive. The two discs are painted alike with eccentric ray or linear patterns, leaving a small white space between each colour. When made to revolve reversely they throw out the most varied and brilliant hues, or seem to contract and expand, according to the way in which they are made to turn. At one moment the spectator is drawn into a whirling vortex and gropes his way along smoothly shining chequered walls dizzily revolving and narrowing towards a constantly turning, constantly opening and closing flower of unearthly splendour for ever beyond his reach; the next instant the movement changes direction and the flower shoots towards him, terrifying in its swollen proportions, thrust forward by the tip of a girating cone which is the vortex pulled inside out. The chromatrope derived from an invention known as the Eidotrope which gave rise to similar effects but without the colour. Two pierced discs revolved in opposite directions, casting projections of continually moving and changing shadow patterns.

Some of the most remarkable lantern effects derive from combinations of the various types of slides. An impressive subject much favoured by Victorian lanternists, who seem to have been immoderately addicted to disasters at sea, was that of a ship foundering in mid-ocean after having been struck by lightning in a fearful storm. The lightning was counterfeited by means of a slipping slide which hid the painted flash and the high lights on the vertiginous waves except for the second when it was drawn aside. The slow, agonized sinking was contrived in the following manner: the sea, a little of the sky, and the lifeboats were painted on one slide, and a second slide consisted of two glasses on one of which was depicted the ship, which could be moved up or down as required, and on the other of which appeared part of the sky and a little of the sea. Each slide formed slightly more than half a circle. When the slide of the ship was raised the vessel disappeared behind the blank half of the other slide. The motion of the doomed ship was controlled by rack and pinion.

The earlier slides were all hand-drawn and -painted, and each one was a unique work of art. Among the latest examples to be made in this way is a set in a private collection painted during the middle years of the nineteenth century and illustrating the story of *Uncle Tom's Cabin*. These glasses, though entirely different in style and spirit—a Pre-Raphaelite concern with precise detail having taken place of the free, expressionist approach of the older slide makers—are drawn with as much vigour and conviction as the central European religious subjects I mentioned a few pages back.

Many exquisitely painted transparencies appeared between 1826 and 1850, the work of Carpenter and Westley, who were also makers of lanterns. Their themes included some historic subjects, such as Napoleon reviewing his troops and the battles of Trafalgar and Waterloo, but they specialized in superb topographical paintings showing Venice, Amsterdam, the Bay of Naples with Vesuvius in eruption, and the Far North illumined by the Midnight Sun. Among their later productions was a series of instructive rack-work slides demonstrating the diurnal motion of the earth and the courses of the planets.

After about 1860 the work began to deteriorate. Engravings and drawings were often transferred to the glasses by photographic means and then coloured. Thus Phiz's illustrations to *Pickwick Papers* were turned into slides, as was a set of comic drawings he did to show the curious shapes of cast shadows, a subject perhaps suggested to him by the hand shadows which were popular at the time both in street shows and private entertainments. The subjects comprise a young dandy whose oval head, thin neck, and butterfly collar throw the shadow of an enormous spoon; two cockneys quarrelling, their shadows forming a saucepan and a kettle above the caption 'The pot calling the kettle black'; a stout lady in a flat hat whose shadow is that of a sheep's head; another lady, holding up an umbrella and leaning backwards in a gale, who makes the silhouette of an elephant; and a skivvy wearing a tall cap and laden with coal and brooms whose monster shadow is that of a negro, the caption reading 'Slave'.

The Raphael cartoons in the Victoria and Albert Museum were photographically transferred to slides and horribly coloured in bright blue and crimson by girls specially employed for that purpose who were usually wholly ignorant of the originals of the subjects they were called upon to paint. They worked in the Toy Theatre tradition, which was delightfully appropriate in the case of trick slides and fairy-tale subjects, but often disastrous and sometimes comic when applied to old masters or views of foreign parts. Engravings of all Landseer's animal paintings were made into a lantern-slide set which could be purchased either plain or coloured. Leech's seaside drawings furnished another set; and countless individual engravings and drawings were reproduced, sometimes to be shown singly, sometimes to be used indiscriminately in any sequence where they appeared to fit. Cruikshank's allegorical drawing of the consequences of drink occurs in any number of the many sets directed against drunkenness; it even turns up in a long moral tale called *The Trial of Sir Jasper* as a portrait of the villain. News items, such as incidents from the Crimean War or the Indian Mutiny, were often reproduced from the pictures in *The Illustrated London News*.

In many of the later mass-produced glasses the Toy Theatre tradition was abandoned in favour of the most repellently anaemic colour range the lantern-slide painter's palette could muster. Striking evidence of the decline in colour is provided by a comparison of the rich glass paintings made during the early Victorian period, from the popular set of engravings of the *Death of Nelson*, with the slides of the same engravings produced photographically some fifty years later and tinted with about as much intensity as a polite young lady's water-colour.

A better impression is made by some of the slides printed by chromolithography. Chromolithography was patented as early as 1837 by Engelmann, a pupil of Senefelder, but was not widely used in England before the 1840's, and not applied to slides until some twenty years later, when it was introduced by J. Theobald and Co., who issued sets of twelve slides, the subjects including topographical scenes, nursery tales, and episodes from the Scriptures.

Transfer printing also occasionally produced good results. A sequence entitled *The Firemen*, of which, to judge from the frequency with which sets are still found, a large number of copies must have been printed, is particularly successful as a series of powerful images. The opening slide shows a messenger arriving at the fire station with news of a terrible conflagration. The men set out; their horses, delineated with tremendous gusto, charge with steaming nostrils along the dark streets towards an orange glow reflected in the moonlit sky. When they reach the blaze the animals rear up in terror, knocking down a passer-by, and a remarkable close-up shows their tossing manes and mad eyes against a background of leaping flame, purple and white-hot with the prey it has already consumed. The scenes of the firemen rescuing women and children, climbing up through the great tongues of fire and the belching smoke, making their way across burning roof-tops and along collapsing rafters, and finally receiving gold medals from a frock-coated, top-hatted gentleman in the station yard, are no less memorable. The dramatic fervour of these pictures is in no way impaired by the fact that very often owing to the rubbing of the transfer some of the scenes seem to be taking place in a thick snow-storm.

From what has been said so far it is clear that the subject-matter of lantern slides became ever more varied as the nineteenth century wore on. The range was as wide as that covered by the film today, comprising sequences taken from popular fiction, topographical themes, news items and historic episodes, comic effects, and even educational series, for many of the slide manufacturers advertised anatomical diagrams and natural history subjects.

Sets of slides with a moral aim preponderated during the last decade of the century, many of them published by the Band of Hope Union and other temperance societies. Popular subjects of this kind included *The Pilgrim's Progress*, 'drawn by Miss Preston', *The Little Captain*, *A Temperance Journey Round the World*, *Abstinence and Hard Work*, and *The Two Roads*. In the latter the hero has to choose between a flowery and a thorny path, the flowery path leading to a wonderful glass-house full of giant ferns, palms, and exotic flowers. *Abstinence and Hard Work*, though consisting in the main of feebly coloured reproductions of bad drawings, opens with an actual photograph which gives the set a strong period flavour. It shows a coster's stall parked outside a public house with the following notice attached to it:

'Children are minded here
Whiles Their parents
As their beer
Id each is all you pay
For 10 minutes
Every day.'

The weak, unconvincing drawing and sentimentality of most of the numerous renderings of biblical subjects present a sad contrast to the early religious slides. Though delineated in careful perspective, with not a single background detail omitted, they are without a spark of vitality and consequently seem utterly dreary and unreal. If only they had been inspired by the stained glass of the period, the merits of which have been strangely overlooked, they might have formed a most interesting counterpart to the slides based on the medieval art of stained glass; but they were for the most part not expressly designed as glass pictures (as successful slides must be) and are of no value except to show the temper of the age. Sets of illustrated hymns were almost as popular and were manufactured in almost as great quantities as the moral tales and Old and New Testament themes. Some of these hymns are charmingly framed in borders of typically Victorian flowers—tiger lilies, striped tulips, freaked dahlias, large cabbage roses, and picotees. Among the few recorded names of the designers of these sets of hymns is that of one Frank Weeks. Each of his slides contained 'a portion of the hymn in large clear type, surrounded by an ingenious tablet design and accompanied by pictorial representations of the subject referred to in the words'. The subjects of Frank Weeks's slides included *Samson, the strongest man From all strong drink abstained, Sad is the Drunkard's Life, How can he leave them,* and *Look not upon the Wine with its Ruby Glow.*

The decline in quality of hand-drawn and painted slides, and the mediocrity of a great many of the slides reproduced from drawings and engravings by photographic means, was probably due in part to the impact of the photographic image itself on the figurative arts and to the increasing popularity of the photograph. But a vast quantity of the purely photographic slides made throughout the last half of the Victorian period are themselves of little interest.

The first public display of photographic slides took place as early as 1858,

Scene from *Rocked in the Cradle of the Deep*, with painted background

Scene from *Ora Pro Nobis*

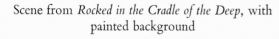

Victorian slides from life models

Scene from *The Bronze Statue*, with painted background

Scene from *Curfew Shall Not Ring Tonight*

Joe prays for faithless Annie, from *Ostler Joe*

Scene from *Children of the City*

Victorian slides from life models

Scene from *Sisters of Light*

Scene from *The Drunkard's Return*

and from then onwards photographic slides were included among the productions of most slide makers. Amateurs were encouraged to make their own photographic slides, and it is this which perhaps accounts for the unconnected subjects so often encountered in surviving collections and for the drabness of so many of the pictures. For, in fact, the best of the Victorian photographic slides must rank among the most exciting images ever projected by the lantern. The subjects were at first topographical and instructive, embracing all parts of England, the Empire, America, and Europe, and such themes as *Magnetism and Electricity*, *All About a London Daily*, *Miners and Mining*, *Microscopic Gems*, *Parasites and their Hosts*, *Human Physiology*, *The Heart and How it Beats*. Portrait studies were also favoured, especially of the Royal Family or of heroes such as General Gordon, and there were also, as we shall see, outstanding photographic depictions of tales and illustrations to songs.

The widespread popularity of the lantern-show entertainment in the latter half of the nineteenth century is proved not only by the multitudes of slides still in existence but by the facts that 'Optical Lantern Entertainments' were given daily at the Crystal Palace throughout the eighties and nineties and that twenty-eight firms were engaged in the manufacture of lanterns and slides in London alone. Two of the slide publishers, Walter Tyler, who was established in the Waterloo Road, and W. G. Hughes, maker of the 'Bijou Malden Triple' lantern, of 82 Mortimer Road, Kingsland, ran exhibition galleries where thousands of glasses were on view, those made by Mr. Hughes being described in his catalogue as 'the most chaste and beautifully executed Slides and Effects'. Most of the firms made and sold viewers, very much like those used today for looking at colour transparencies, so that slides could be examined without having to be projected. They were usually constructed of mahogany, with eye-pieces which could be adjusted by means of bellows and screws. An inclined mirror behind the slide created an effect recalling that of the Vienna peepshows, and brought out the full brilliance of the slide when held directly beneath a light or in strong sunshine.

If they were not made at home, slides, like Toy Theatre prints, could be purchased either plain or coloured, and for those enthusiasts who wished to colour their own glasses special boxes of slide-painting pigments and flat wedge-shaped brushes were provided for the sum of thirty shillings. There were several manuals of instruction to help them, among the most frequently advertised being that by Edward Groom and *The Book of the Lantern* by T. C. Hepworth. Transparent colours only could be used, so the range was limited. It included gamboge, Italian pink, gallstone, Indian yellow, madder lake, crimson lake, Prussian blue (a very favourite colour), indigo, burnt Sienna, brown madder, Vandyke brown, and lampblack.

The original lanterns used by the wandering showmen were small and simple, with plain bodies of japanned tin, and they were generally illumined only with candles. But as the lantern show developed into a large-scale entertainment the apparatus became more complicated. Effects of movement were contrived not only by the slides but by the projectors themselves. Lanterns also grew more flamboyant in appearance. 'It is well to have the lantern as showy as possible', writes a professional lanternist in 1858, 'to make a good impression.'

The chimney of a mid-nineteenth-century French lantern of Russian iron in the Barnes Collection is capped by a fluted cone and a broad ornamental ring, while the body is surmounted by an amusing fretted cornice of half-classic, half-Gothic design and adorned with beaded panels enclosing pretty star and circle patterns. Some lanterns were still fashioned of japanned tin, but these were the least prized and the least expensive. The more popular projectors were of Russian iron or of seasoned mahogany lined with Russian iron. The 'Optimus' magic lantern, manufactured by Perken, Son, and Rayment, and advertised as suitable for the drawing-room, was of polished mahogany with panelled doors and lacquered brass fittings and stood on an elaborate moulded foot. Chimneys were finished not only with single- but with double- and triple-fluted cones like piled metal pie frills. The chimney of Chadwick's 'Perfect' lantern sported a Greek key pattern in black, white, and gold enamel.

For illumination, candles and the simple oil lamp were replaced by improved oil lights, by gas and limelight and, at the end of the century, by electricity. Foremost among the improved oil lanterns were the 'Pamphengos' (Hughes's patent), the 'Sciopticon', the first of its kind, and Archer's 'Photinus'. They all burnt with a pure white light, were provided with four wicks, which were flat instead of round, and made use of heat-resisting conoidal glasses.

Limelight was produced by impinging a flame resulting from the combustion of oxygen and hydrogen gas against a cylinder of hard lime, the gas being stored in rubber bags or metal containers; and many special gadgets were devised to control this illuminant which could prove highly dangerous. There was difficulty in adjusting it so that it neither overheated the lantern nor imparted a yellow tinge to the image. The hiss of the jets, moreover, though a sign that all was well, was all too often a distracting influence. Mr. Chadwick's 'Perfect' lantern, already mentioned, seems to have been one of the more reputable and reliable projectors for use with limelight.

In order that the slides might be changed smoothly and easily, an apparatus known as a 'Metamorphoser' was used. It consisted of two slide-holders one above the other, either of which could be brought in front of the condenser, slowly or quickly, by moving a lever. With the aid of another gadget, 'Beard's Eclipse' carrier, the slide next to be shown was passed in front of the one showing and the latter could be instantly withdrawn to the same side at which it was put on, while the former was pressed into focus by means of a spring. There was also an ingenious contrivance called the 'Terpuoscope' which gave the appearance of an opaque curtain descending on the screen each time the slide was changed, while yet another arrangement entitled 'Lancaster's Shutter' darkened the whole of the picture at the same time instead of allowing the shadow to appear first on one side of the image and then on the other, as with the ordinary sliding shutter.

When pictures were to be exhibited in swift succession to create the impression of a moving panorama the action was controlled by an endless band and a steel spring. And finally, in order to dissolve one view into another, so that one picture faded gradually away as another took its place, two lanterns were placed side by side, or two or even three lenses, one above the other, were combined in a single lantern. The lenses were so adjusted that the projected images perfectly coincided and thus one picture could be made to merge imperceptibly into another, creating a distinct sense of movement. A common effect achieved by this means was the change from day into night or winter into summer, effected by two slides of the same scene at different times of the day or season. The transformation of a black and white photograph of a vase of flowers into a picture in full colour was also managed by means of two lenses.

In the days before electricity was available the control of the illuminant for biunial and triple lanterns was a tricky business. The light had to be turned up to its full height in one lantern before that in the other began to diminish. The difficulty was overcome by what was called a dissolver, or dissolving taps, the commonest form of this gadget being the 'Star' dissolver. Biunial and triple lanterns were manufactured by many firms during the last thirty years of the nineteenth century, prominent among them being Walter Tyler, W. C. Hughes, and Riley Brothers of Bradford. During the nineties a 'Leviathan' automatic lantern was produced (Allen's patent), 'made in the very highest style throughout', which was illumined by electric light and was guaranteed to show fifty slides in less than two minutes.

The popular public shows of late Victorian times were all given with biunial or triple lanterns. A notable exhibitor of the period was C. Goodwin Norton, the author of a widely distributed treatise on the lantern and a maker of lanterns and every kind of slide, both reproductions of drawn and engraved images and pure photographs. The main part of a characteristic Goodwin Norton magic-lantern show was taken up with topographical views, though illustrations to some well-known poem, usually by either Browning or Tennyson, might form part of the programme, and a fairy-tale might be added if there were children in the audience. After 1896 Goodwin Norton used a cinematograph as well as a lantern and followed the projection of a series of slides with 'animated pictures'.

It is abundantly clear from his book that his principal interest was in the mechanism of his apparatus, in the creation of rapid changes and illusions. He liked to open a programme with a view of a country cottage by day, dissolving the daylight into moonlight and then cloaking the scene in a snow-storm. He showed the Houses of Parliament in the beams of a slowly rising moon which rippled across the surface of the river; and in the last of his series of slides showing the Hôtel de Ville, Paris, the windows of the great house would light up one by one as night drew on. From his choice of subject it is obvious that he was among those many earnest Victorians who strove to combine pleasure with instruction, and this is borne out both by his own photograph in the Science Museum and by his contemptuous reference to comic slip slides: 'The lanternist will do well to avoid these altogether, unless showing to mere children.'

Goodwin Norton's contemporary, D. W. Noakes, some of whose slides were shown in London at the National Film Theatre and at the Lyric Theatre,

Hammersmith, in 1961, was a bird of different feather, far more of a popular showman, out, above all things, to attract large audiences. Like so many of the characters encountered in the business of showing moving pictures, Noakes was very versatile. He was official photographer for the Thames Conservancy Board, in which capacity he was responsible for photographing all the wrecks on the Thames, pursuing this occupation in the same unsavoury waters and in much the same manner as Gaffer Hexham was wont to follow his more sinister business with wrecked and drowned humanity. Noakes owned Hays Wharf in Greenwich and supplied hay for the London bus horses; he became Mayor of Greenwich; and he was in addition to all this an engineer of considerable ability: when the lift at one end of the Greenwich Tunnel broke down, he repaired a 6 ft. fracture in its hydraulic cylinder with such ingenuity that he was considered to have created a record in the annals of engineering.

It is of interest, in the light of the earlier history of lantern projection, to know that Noakes was particularly attracted by trick effects of all kinds and that one of his sons, Ernest, became Vice-President of the Magic Circle and set up a workshop in Greenwich where he made all the properties used by members of the Circle. He also wrote a book entitled *Magical Originalities* in which many of his own and his father's inventions are described.

Noakes exhibited before royalty at the Albert Hall, and advertised a show given at the Crystal Palace throughout the second half of April 1891 as a 'new and original Dioramic entertainment', though in fact it had nothing in common with the Diorama and did not differ in principle from the triple-lantern exhibitions which had been common for at least twenty years.

Noakes's apparatus, to which he gave the name of 'Noakesoscope', was merely a quadruple instead of a triple lantern; he used it, however, in conjunction with a dissolver of his own invention, the 'Gem', which enabled him to make play with all four lanterns in any order or combination; and he furthermore excited public attention by projecting his slides on to a screen far larger than that hitherto seen at any lantern display. It measured 1,700 sq. ft.

The show Noakes gave at the Crystal Palace was marked, too, by a certain originality, for, like a modern film entertainment, it concentrated on one particular theme instead of showing a series of disconnected items of equal importance such as made up the usual lantern-slide programme of the period. Noakes had built for himself at Hays Wharf a steam launch, the *Lizzie*, and had the novel idea of travelling on it through the canals of England, taking photographs as he went. He covered six hundred miles and produced two hundred and twenty photographs. He made these into slides, coloured them, and showed them under the title *England Bisected by a Steam Launch*. As one picture dissolved into another through the agency of the smoothly working Noakesoscope, the viewers felt as though they were aboard the *Lizzie* gliding through the prettily tinted countryside unfolding in enchanting variety on their either hand.

Yet though Noakes showed enterprise enough in promoting this show, and though his sequence of slides was longer and more comprehensive than any similar series, the subject was not entirely new. Two years previously W. B. Horner and Son, who were among the most prolific manufacturers of slides, were advertising photographic sets entitled *Round the World in a Yacht* and *Round the World with a Camera*, *Up the Rhine*, and *Down the Wye*. The quality of Horner's slides, too, was superior to that of Noakes's, as was that of Goodwin Norton's superb topographical studies. Noakes's slides were charmingly but feebly coloured, whereas some of Horner's glasses had a Gauguinesque richness.

Photographic slides were in general much more vigorously coloured than the drawn slides of the late Victorian period; and when the colourists were presented with photographic scenes of which they had no knowledge, instead of producing something tasteless, as they nearly always did when they were confronted with a reproduction of a masterpiece of painting, they gave full reign to their imagination and turned factual records into exotic, haunting visions.

Noakes did not preside in person at the Crystal Palace shows; the Noakesoscope was worked by Mr. C. W. Locke and the performance was accompanied by incidental music played on the organ by Mr. Henry Watson. Despite all that was claimed for it, the display was little noticed in the Press and could not have enjoyed an unqualified success, for it was not repeated after Saturday May 2nd, 1891, even though there were fifteen hundred free seats for every performance and the charge for reserved seats was only sixpence.

The two Noakesoscope displays given in London during 1961, poor though many of the slides were, gave modern audiences a splendid opportunity of witnessing the kind of show enjoyed by the Victorians and of experiencing some of the astonishing effects of which the multiple lanterns, triple or quadruple, were capable. One of the programmes was almost identical with that given at the Crystal Palace seventy years previously; the other consisted of a variety of slides such as formed the usual repertoire of Victorian lantern showmen. Many of these were badly coloured reproductions of tenth-rate drawings and engravings, but they included some fine portraits of the Queen, and the show concluded with a delightful series of sculptures from the Great Exhibition, each revealed by the slow raising of a pink curtain. And finally there was a ravishing effect of seasonal change and of day melting into night which must have been very similar to Goodwin Norton's country-cottage scene.

The slides in this series were of a different order from most of the rest, carefully painted with a fine feeling for colour and solidity. First a gabled Victorian cottage was shown on the edge of a wood in the full light of a summer noon. The daylight waned, night fell, a lamp shone from the windows of the little house. The darkness grew pitchy, the lamp was extinguished, the full shapes of the trees almost vanished in the encircling gloom, then the full moon rose.

There was a pause, such as only the lantern can accomplish, richly charged with silence and suspense. Then very gently snow began to fall. (This was contrived in the traditional manner of the lanternist by means of a piece of opaque calico pricked with holes and wound about two rollers. As the calico was passed upwards on to the top roller, the snow appeared to fall across the scene.) When day dawned the cottage was mantled in white. The trees, bending under the snow and icicle-fringed, had lost their leaves. And still the flakes fell. Christmas came and carol-singers (a row of tiny figures on an opaque ground pushed across the lens) moved stiffly up to the cottage door. A red blind in the parlour window rolled up to reveal a family sitting round the fire. When the singers had gone the blind was lowered, the light in the cottage went out, and the darkness was unbroken except for the sparkle of a solitary star. Christmas Day dawned, white, clear and frosty, to the sound of wild church bells.

7

Living Models

All the parts are made to tend to a dramatic whole, each picture
dependent on the other and all the details illustrative of the complete
work; the same characters recur again and again, moved in different
tableaux with varied passions, one moral running through all; the
beginning finding its natural climax in the end. Another novelty is
the wonderful way in which all the objects in the picture tend to
illustrate the story.

REDGRAVE

IN THE previous chapter passing reference was made to photographic slides
illustrating fiction and song. This group, much less well known today than all
other forms of slides, was never included in the Crystal Palace displays regularly
advertised in the London newspapers and seems to have been ignored by
lanternists such as Goodwin Norton and David Noakes. Yet viewed as social
documents they are more impressive than any of the material which has been
discussed here, while as images they surpass all other varieties of slides, for they
create a new mode of vision. The imaginative use of photography conspired
with painting and the magic of projection to produce an impact of which
academic painting was no longer capable by the end of the last century, and
which the factual photograph, with all its power of transfixing momentary,
casual effects, could never achieve.

These remarkable slides immediately preceded the cinema as a form of
popular entertainment, and employed many of the devices which we are
inclined to regard as peculiar to the film, particularly the flash-back and the
convincing presentation of the fantastic. The powerful sequence with close-ups

of a wild-haired girl swinging on the clapper of a great church bell in *Curfew Shall Not Ring Tonight* anticipates the breathtaking leaping and rope-swinging feats of Douglas Fairbanks. The surrealist visions of Meliès are foreshadowed by poetic compositions such as that in *Rocked in the Cradle of the Deep*, of the pallid sailor boy stretched by an anchor on the floor of the ocean, entangled in weed, eyed by curious fish, and with a recording angel at his side; or that in *What are the Wild Waves Saying?* of a bedroom wall dissolving to reveal a stormy sea crushing a mighty ship as though it were a matchbox and threatening to engulf the occupants of the room, a brother and sister asleep on a little iron bedstead, then merging into an idyllic landscape with a mountain river rushing down from rocky heights to join the ocean, all its turbulence smoothed into a wide, glassy expanse as fresh water meets salt.

Like the film, these slides are composed from living models placed against an actual scene or a painted set, and as in the early cinema the impulse behind them is purely visual so that they work their magic with scripts which more often than not have nothing to recommend them as works of art. The idea of using life models and photography to interpret a work of imagination was not new. An American, John Jabez Edwin Mayall, who came to London from Philadelphia in 1846, had shown several sets of daguerrotypes of this kind at the Great Exhibition. They included ten daguerrotypes illustrating the Lord's Prayer, a series of six based on *The Soldier's Dream* by Campbell, and an invention entitled *The Venerable Bede blessing an Anglo-Saxon Child*. In some of these, as in many of the lantern slides, painted landscape backgrounds appeared behind the models, while in others a landscape was painted on to the photograph.

For some fifteen or twenty years after Mayall's exhibition, however, the makers of lantern slides went on issuing hand-painted glasses or transparencies of mechanically reproduced drawings and engravings to translate tales and verse into projected images, although, as we have seen, they made use of photographs for topographical and documentary subjects. The pioneer in the employment of life models for slides was probably Joseph Bamforth of Holmfirth, Yorkshire, who began to supply glasses made in this way before the sixties were out. He would prepare his photographs by making a preliminary sketch, and would then pose his models, who were always local people. His backgrounds were nearly always painted though he often made use of 'props'—

rugs, a plush sofa, a richly patterned tablecloth, a landscape picture of a river flowing beneath a chalky cliff, a print of a fat little girl by Landseer, and a battered church organ, very useful for conjuring up a telling vision of Paradise with music-making angels, and indispensable in the several versions of *The Lost Chord*; one or more of these objects appear in story after story.

When Bamforth's life models, as sometimes happens, are imposed on the background photograph of an actual scene, curious errors in perspective are apt to occur which often, to our delighted eyes, trained as they are by the aesthetic 'isms' of our century, enhance the compelling, surrealist atmosphere of the projected picture. In *The Curtain*, for instance, the foreground is occupied by a young woman in white muslin who looks through a raised curtain into the past and the future. One scene is of a bedroom in which a woman is reduced to knee height by the giant bed and advances towards it at the totally unnatural angle seen only in dreams or in the paintings of a Max Ernst or a Chagall. Two bowler-hatted gentlemen walking towards the camera in *Three Little Wise Men* are much shorter than the villagers in the street behind them, and look like stunted dwarfs from a circus instead of the prosperous squires they are intended to represent.

Bamforth's example was soon followed by many other slide makers. Their names are not always known, for they were rarely in the habit of advertising themselves on the title slide of the sequences as Joseph Bamforth often did. Few of their glasses surpass those made at Holmfirth, though numbers of fine sets were produced by Riley Brothers, W. G. Hughes, Horner, Middleton, W. H. Humphries, Dunscombe of Bristol, and by some of the temperance societies.

The application of photography to the manufacture of narrative slides and the introduction of living models endowed the projected image with a more vivid human interest, a form of realism more readily intelligible to the unsophisticated, and a wider emotional range than it had so far been able to command. They coincided with the publication of a stream of verse and fiction, prompted, as were most of the slides, by the social conditions of the period, the pressing question of poverty and its attendant evils, drunkenness and depravity.

The problem of poverty had become so acute that it could no longer be ignored as part of a divinely ordered scheme. During the eighties the capital and the larger towns were flooded with emigrants from the country seeking casual unskilled labour, and even London, the most orderly of cities, became the scene of demonstrations which the police were sometimes unable to control. Vast processions of the starving unemployed culminated in 1887 in 'Bloody Sunday'. There were in swift succession attempts to bomb Westminster Hall, the House of Commons, the Tower, London Bridge, Nelson's Column, and three of the railway stations—disturbances which had little concrete result, but which concentrated interest on the nightmarish circumstances in which at least a tenth of the population of Britain passed their lives, utterly destitute and degraded if they were unable to find work and sweated and exploited if they were employed, doomed all too often to pass the whole of their lives in surroundings of such misery and squalor that only the strongest among them could resist the wretched consolation offered by the gin palace.

Scores of minor popular writers were moved to focus attention on this scene of distress and to offer the comforts of religion and right living to the sufferers. Prominent among them were Mrs. O. F. Walton, whose *Peep behind the Scenes*, *Christie's Old Organ*, *Nobody Loves Me*, and *The Mysterious House* rang the changes on the themes of Ruin, Redemption, and Regeneration; Amy Le Feuvre, best known for her *Probable Sons*, an application to everyday life of the parable of the Prodigal Son, miscalled 'Probable' by the little heroine, and for *Teddy's Button*, which contains a surprisingly lively picture of two children within its sugary frame; Hesba Stretton, whose name is perhaps less familiar than her best-seller *Jessica's First Prayer*, yet who was among the few of this type of writer to be recommended by the subscription libraries; Mercy Stratton, responsible for *Engine Bill* and *The Two Sovereigns*; Fanny Eden, a great favourite, whose *White Slaves of London* reads like a mawkish adaptation of Dickens's description of Bleeding Heart Yard, and who also wrote *Nobody's Darling*, and *Not Wanted* in which occurs the famous song *Father Come Home*; L. E. Tiddemann, who addressed his *Poverty's Pupil* expressly to working girls, the pupil being the motherless daughter of a drunkard and thus particularly exposed to temptation; Josh Hainsworth; H. Fitzgerald; Sydney Watson, who concentrated on tales of destitute city orphans such as *Wops the Waif* and *Shag and Doll;* and the Rev. Silas Hocking, author of a charming little fantasy called *Dick's Fairy*.

The most robust of these well-meaning, if sentimental, story-tellers and versifiers was George R. Sims, whose sense of the melodramatic, as well as his strong compassion, provided the slide makers with ideal material. He had first-hand knowledge of his subject, for the series of articles he wrote for the *Pictorial World*, entitled 'How the Poor Live', was based on months of exploration of the poor and criminal areas of South and East London in the company of a School Board officer, Arthur B. Ross, whom he had met when addressing the Sunday gathering of a Radical club in Southwark. *The Dagonet Ballads*, some of which were written before, some after, the visits with Mr. Ross, and which were published in the seventies, were concerned with the suffering of the poor and also with the immorality of which poverty was the cause. They at once established Sims as a champion of the down-trodden. *Christmas Day in the Workhouse* and *Billy's Rose* were denounced as mischievous attempts to set the paupers against their betters, while *Ostler Joe*, which was recited at an amateur entertainment in Washington (where it was attributed to Swinburne!), was reported in the *New York Times* as having 'distressed and deeply embarrassed every man and woman in the chosen audience that had listened to those indecent verses'.

These verses tell how Ostler Joe's wife, fair Annie, is seduced by a wealthy city scoundrel, leaves her husband and child for a life of shame, and is reunited on her deathbed to the faithful, honest Joe.

'In his arms death found her lying, in his arms her spirit fled,
And his tears came down in torrents as he knelt beside her dead.
Never once his love had faltered through her base unhallowed life;
And the stone above her ashes bears the honoured name of wife.'

It was this last, that Annie should not only be loved and forgiven but should still enjoy the name of wife, which shocked respectable people.

But among the poor, for whom they were made, Bamforth's slides depicting this story were as much in demand as the striking sets illustrating most of the other Dagonet ballads: *The Matron's Story, In the Harbour, The Lifeboat, Billy's Rose, Christmas Day in the Workhouse, A Sister's Story, Nellie's Prayer, The Street Tumblers, One Winter Night, Orinska, In the Signal Box*, and *The Level Crossing*.

The public to whom most of this literature was explicitly addressed was still largely illiterate; the older ideal of education based on religion and the teaching of hereditary crafts in the home had vanished with the immigration into the towns; only the most rudimentary instruction in reading, writing, and arithmetic had taken its place, and even elementary education was not compulsory before 1880 or free to all until 1891. It seems likely, therefore, that the thousands of slides based on these and similar writings, and the lantern readings taken from them, were inspired by the need to communicate to illiterate audiences.

The slides were produced in sets varying in number from five or six to as many as sixty, and they were exhibited in towns all over the country to working-class people at meetings sponsored by the Church Mission Society, the Religious Tract Society, the Church of England Temperance Society, the Band of Hope, and similar groups. Admission usually cost sixpence, though sometimes no entrance charge was made and there was a collection at the end of the show.

Despite the serious intentions of the promoters of these displays, they were looked upon as entertainments and indeed played much the same part in the lives of those who attended them as the cinema was to do twenty and thirty years later. The programmes consequently showed a tendency to expand to embrace subjects which had no direct bearing on contemporary problems and conditions. Historical themes such as Mary, Queen of Scots and Lady Jane Grey were introduced and the repertoire was increased by adaptations from well-known novels such as *The Cricket on the Hearth*, *The Old Curiosity Shop*, Mrs. Hungerford's *Molly Bawn* and Miss Bradon's *Sir Jasper's Tenant*; the illustrated religious songs, such as *Ora Pro Nobis* and *The Lost Chord*, which were conspicuous in the earlier productions, became intermingled with sets of glasses picturing favourite secular verse and song, such as *Excelsior*, *The Village Blacksmith*, *Robin Adair*, *The Scent of the Lilies*, *What are the Wild Waves Saying?* *Beautiful Garden of Roses* by J. Dempsey, *Sing me to Sleep*, *Eileen Allanagh*, *Kathleen Mavourneen*, and *The Girl Behind the Counter*.

Regarded as social documents, the slides dealing with the conditions of the poor and the evils of drink are as vivid and as moving as Mayhew's recorded interviews with London workers, outcasts, and vagabonds which had taken place some thirty years earlier. Sets such as *The White Slaves of London*, *The Street Arabs of London*, *Wops the Waif*, *Nell*, *Poor Mike*, *In Darkest London*, *Shag and Doll*, and *The Toilers* transform the thin, flat, insipid narratives from which they derive into unforgettable images of the misery which we know existed but which we seldom visualize with the full clarity of unpalatable detail with which it is revealed here.

The Street Arabs of London pictures the state of hooliganism produced by a combination of abject poverty and the decay of apprenticeship. The slides show the almost insurmountable difficulties encountered by the clergymen and philanthropists who only partially succeeded in checking these gangs of boys and establishing clubs for them by resorting to a more muscular form of Christianity than that generally practised by their contemporaries. In *Kitty*, a story by an anonymous author, a poor factory girl, brought up by a dissolute drunken old woman, attends a breakfast at a Salvation Army hostel, a scene which depicts more graphically than any historical document what it meant to be born poor eighty years ago.

The White Slaves of London introduces us to a tenement in one of the foulest districts of the city. A matchbox maker, haggard and ill clad, works in a damp, dark garret from dawn till midnight assisted by a pale, crippled boy lying on a heap of filthy rags; another woman, far too old to work by our standards, sews sacks in a room of even greater squalor. The exquisite colours of the scene—the rich plum of the stained, peeling walls, the browns and rusty blacks of the bowed figure, the tawny sacks—only heighten our response to its sad significance. The impact of another interior is still more poignant. Two sisters are seen making shirts by the side of their crazed old mother. These workers, unlike the others, are neatly dressed, their humble lodging is spotless, and on the window-ledge, between fresh, looped muslin, stands a pot of scarlet geraniums, a dim reminder in the midst of this dreadful slum of the sight and touch of growing nature, the birthright of which all who are trapped in the tenement have been deprived. Other sets of slides show starved children dying from exposure, injured in street accidents, cowering in vile hovels, seeking shelter among the slimy piers of a derelict wharf, sweeping crossings or ganging up to pick pockets.

The scenes are depicted with such intensity of feeling and so powerful a use of the medium that it is impossible to doubt the reality of the experiences which gave rise to them. The fact that no practical remedy for these ills is suggested, that the abhorred workhouse is the only refuge from them, adds to the horror and compassion they inspire. The only comfort offered to the poor mother in *The White Slaves of London* when her child dies of hunger and neglect is a glimpse of heaven's pearly gates and a flimsy vision of the Saviour accompanied by angels with white paper wings. A similar apparition is supposed to console a deserted mother lying on a dirty pile of straw with five starving babies, and to sustain the famished heroine of *One Winter Night* as she sinks to her death in the snow after strangling her ailing child.

The contrast between the sentimentality of the religious palliative and the inexorable conditions pictured by the slides is painful to a modern viewer. Resignation is the message of these harrowing tales, resignation with the possibility, in the case of drunkenness, of slightly improved circumstances through abstention and regular attendance at a place of worship.

One interesting aspect of the slides to present-day spectators is that although they are undoubtedly intended to draw attention to the plight of the poor, they do not reveal a trace of class consciousness in the political sense. Class is something which is there like the rest of the phenomenal world, and happiness is to be attained, if at all, only by right living and strict adherence to the path and station ordained by God for each living creature. It is proper for the rich to dispense charity, but the circus girl, Betsy Ann, in *A Peep Behind the Scenes*, must not aspire to become more than a kitchen maid, and the poor shirt maker achieves the prescribed limit of her ambitions when she obtains the post of seamstress to a wealthy young woman.

With each set of slides a booklet was issued from which the illustrated story or verse was read aloud, the text being divided into passages corresponding to the slides. Very often the programme incorporated a hymn or a song, the words of which would be flashed on to the screen so that the audience could join in, accompanied by the harmonium or the piano. A printed leaflet advertising an entertainment of this kind given at the Mission Hall, Kettering, in January 1892, together with the actual slides shown and the readings, make it possible to conjure up a clear idea of a lantern evening with glasses produced from life models.

As soon as the viewers had taken their seats and the doors of the hall were closed, the gas-lamps were slowly extinguished, the harmonium sounded, and the lantern flung its beam on to a curtain of dark red velvet that hung over the screen. The curtain lifted to display the picture of a youth raising his bowler (the height of fashion for 1889) to a young woman in a bustle, while the words 'Good Evening' in rustic twig lettering appeared above a background of oak trees. Then followed *Robin Adair*, a curtain-raiser of but half a dozen slides, passed in front of the lens as the audience sang the well-known song. This short sequence introduces us to scenes of affluence. The deserted heroine, ashen pale, sits in a carpeted room with lofty windows, and as she bows her head in agonized recollection of past happiness, a wall of the apartment dissolves to show the ball, the debonair Robin twirling his moustaches among white-clad ladies, palms, and pillars. Those who wondered at this fabulous composition on that winter night in Kettering seventy years ago, transported for a moment from their own drab circumstances, probably failed to note a detail which strikes us forcibly today: with his splendid evening dress Robin wears cracked, broken-down boots. Bamforth took a broad view of production.

This was a double-feature programme and while the lanternist was preparing for one of the main pictures his assistant projected a monochrome photograph of a vase of Christmas roses and changed it imperceptibly by means of a dissolver into a fully coloured image as fine in detail as any flower-piece by Brussel or Huysum. The screen then showed an advertisement for Beecham's Pills: a drawn picture of a curly-haired child holding up a pill-box.

Then the curtain fell. In the darkness a man's voice was heard reciting the opening lines of a narrative poem called *Jane Conquest*, written by Mr. James Milne of Newcastle and originally published in *The Methodist Family*:

' 'Twas about the time of Christmas and many years ago,
When the sky was black with wrath and rack, and the earth was
white with snow,
When loudly rang the tumult of winds and waves at strife,
In her house by the sea with her child on her knee, sat Harry
Conquest's wife.'

At these words the curtain went up to disclose Jane Conquest, a strong-featured, sturdy young woman in a red shawl, seated with her sick child on her lap by a cheerless grate in a cottage interior with a Gothic stone hearth and a latticed window. The tearing, whistling crescendo and diminuendo of a great storm almost drowned the voice of the narrator and a distant, blood-curdling cry. The window was crimsoned with the flickering reflection of a fire (lantern effect), and the next slide, flashed on with lightning speed, showed Jane starting up to the casement. The cottage wall dissolved to reveal a ship in flames not far from the wintry shore. Jane was sole witness of this dreadful sight, the only villager astir to hear the despairing shouts of the victims.

In the next slide she was on her knees praying for strength and inspiration to save the trapped mariners. The strains of 'Abide with me' pealed forth from the harmonium and a plump angel appeared by the cot of the dying child. Jane commended the boy to the care of this celestial being, and, rising to her feet, went out into the frozen night. She fought her way at last through blinding snow to the church on the cliff above the burning vessel (two spectacular slides in which the minute figure of the heroine is seen first in a vast, hostile, white landscape and then on the heights by the church where the wintry waste is unnaturally illumined by the burst of scarlet and orange flames in the mountainous seas). Unable to open the heavy door, Jane climbed through a window, reached the belfry, and grasped the rope, 'sole cord of hope'. The clamour of an actual bell deafened the Kettering audience, ringing on and on until the image of a lifeboat plunging through the breakers showed that help was near, and the reciter confirmed that the rescuers

'O'ercame each check and reached the wreck and saved the hapless
crew.'

But what of the ringer in the belfry? The succeeding slide revealed her motionless and cold upon the floor, the bell-rope still in her icy hand. Meanwhile, by a strange coincidence, Harry Conquest was among those brought off the burning ship, and he was seen making his feeble way, his clothes all scorched and rent, amid overhanging crags, to his snowbound cottage. No light, no fire, no wife were there to welcome him, and poor Harry sank fainting beside the cold hearth and his dying son.

The scene faded and its place was taken by the belfry interior dominated by the large figure of the sexton, his face buried in false whiskers, bending over Jane's unconscious form. He revived her and led her home, where she was astonished and overjoyed to find her husband

'sav'd in that fearful hour
By his wife's brave deed and trust in need in Heaven's all gracious
power.'

As husband and wife embrace each other the child whom Jane had left at death's door was seen to be quietly sleeping, smiling and rosy. A vision of the angel was shown once more behind the cot. The curtain fell as the narrator spoke the concluding words of the poem:

'And this is the Christmas story that still the children tell
Of the fearful sight that winter night and the ringing of the bell.'

Before the applause had died away the curtain rose again and the spectators read an announcement wreathed about by bluebells and sparrows that there was to be an interval of five minutes. After that lapse of time all eyes were once more riveted to the screen by the title of the next tale, '*Dan Dabberton's Dream* by Rev. Frederic Langbridge from Life Models', framed in a circle of ivy leaves and conventionalized roses.

Seen first carousing in the taproom of the Hen and Chickens, Dan Dabberton, a handsome but unkempt, already bald, and bleary-eyed fellow, is clearly a victim of the bottle. His conscience is awakened by a severe-looking stranger singing a new version of 'Home, Sweet Home' with the refrain 'Home, home, dark, dark home! Where father's a drunkard the house is not home', which was echoed softly on the harmonium throughout the reading of the tale.

The landlord and most of his patrons are not favourably impressed by this song, but Dan tears himself from their company. As he lurches homewards, he hears church bells ringing and children singing carols, for it is Christmas Eve. (The harmonium-player imitated the bells and three boys intoned 'While shepherds watched'.) Dan's wife and his little daughter Nellie are not in the poor apartment when he arrives; they have gone to deliver the needlework, their sole means of livelihood, which they have finished just in time for the Festive Season. The humble room is clean and bright, though bare, and after swinging in a drunken stupor on the pendulum of the grandfather clock, the besotted man sinks down beside a cheerful fire. Instantly he falls asleep and the hearth, filling with clouds which gradually roll back to form a frame for visionary scenes, becomes the theatre of Dan's dreams.

His past life flashes before him in a series of brilliant images. The boy is seen at his mother's knee and later at table in an enchanting cottage interior with a flower garden stretching to a blue distance through the open door and a trellised porch. Then all changes. The same interior is denuded of every ornament, stripped of its carpet and most of its furniture. Dan, now a youth, has already succumbed to the demon of drink. The mother, wasted and frail, cringes before the wastrel's violent gestures, and in the background, a vision within a vision, looms the sinister shape of a coffin. It is no surprise to see Dan in the next picture stretched across his mother's newly dug grave.

His grief brings him to his senses; he courts a pretty girl in a red frilled dress in a leafy lane, and leads her home to an elegant house which is in sharp contrast to the poverty-stricken room in the foreground of the scene in which the sleeper lies. Nellie is born and is dandled on her father's arm.

But again temptation is too strong for him. Wife and child shrink at his approach, the pretty parlour is changed for the seedy chamber of the foreground, and then this too vanishes to disclose the bleak ward of a workhouse where Nellie stoops in anguish over the lifeless form of her mother while again the dread coffin hovers near. With a start of terror, Dan awakes to find that the last scene at least is not yet reality and that his wife and child are standing before him. He repents, we hope for the last time, clasps them to his bosom, and the picture ends.

In the Mission Hall at Kettering, as the curtain fell, the harmonium-player struck up a three-part glee, 'Merrily ring the bells', which was sung by the audience. The evening's display was rounded off with a portrait of the Queen in full colour, a hand-lettered slide, patterned like a tile, reading 'Good Night', and an announcement of the time and date of the next week's programme.

We have no record of how those viewers of 1892 reacted to such pictorial material, though the many thousands of slides of a similar character which were produced testify to their popularity. We may be sure, however, that they did not indulge in the laughter which spices our own delight in these melodramas whenever, as in the programme just described, we are not made so sharply aware of the terrible conditions which gave rise to them. It is probable, too, that the Victorian audience took for granted the amazing vitality of the images, which is what most astonishes and excites a modern spectator.

The idea of superimposing one photograph on another and combining photographs, which is exploited with such admirable fantasy by the slide makers, did not originate with them. Combination photographs had first been made by Gustave Le Gray, a former painter and the pupil of Paul Delaroche. And striking examples of composite landscapes and figure subjects with a high moral tone were produced by C. Silvry in France and in England by O. G. Rejlander and H. P. Robinson, both of whom were painters as well as photographers. A photograph made by O. G. Rejlander in 1857, called *The Two Ways of Life*, was built up from thirty negatives and looked like a photographic reproduction of some monumental Renaissance painting. The best of Henry Peach Robinson's combination prints, *Fading Away* (1858) and *Bringing Home the May* (1863), were in the nature of genre pictures. The endeavour of all these photographers was to create a composition which would appear as much like a realistic academic painting as possible.

The slide makers, on the other hand, aimed at a surrealist result far in advance of their time. Joseph Bamforth and his son Edwin were outstanding artists, unrivalled masters indeed, in the creation of visionary pictures within pictures, although Dunscombe of Bristol, who was responsible for *Dan Dabberton's Dream*, also used the technique to great advantage. His conceptions tend on the whole, however, to be more prosaic than those of the Bamforths. In Dunscombe's slides the dream picture always has some sort of framework, such as the hearth in *Dan Dabberton's Dream*, and is seen as precisely as the real figures and objects in the foreground of the composition. Joseph and Edwin Bamforth's phantasms merge into the actual scene, dissolving at the edges into semi-transparent, rainbow-hued mist which veils but does not hide the appurtenances of common day. *What are the Wild Waves Saying?* and *Robin Adair*, both of which have already been mentioned, are particularly haunting examples of the process, and it also plays a vital part in the poetic *Scent of the Lilies*.

Here a portly, pompous, elderly man sits in a massively appointed parlour clutching in his podgy hand a lily (fresh as ever) given him by his long-dead love. Suddenly, as he thinks sadly of the past, just above the table draped in mulberry-coloured plush, on which he leans his elbow, there floats an apparition of himself in youth, clad in a striped jacket, kneeling at the feet of a girl in muslin in a sylvan glade by a winding river. As he looks, the vision changes and the tragic tale of his ill-starred passion is gradually unfolded.

In *The Heavenly City* the wall behind a woman lying on a sofa melts into a perspective of exotic onion domes and a citadel peopled by winged beings, and this then gives way to a cellarous interior where an angel, looking accusingly at the woman, points to a group of starving children.

In *Love Me and the World is Mine* the trite words of the song have inspired a compelling, romantic composition. The dark figure of a youth half kneels by a gate in the foreground close to the ivy-grown hulk of a stricken willow, his face turned away from us towards a landscape of water-meadows and streams where a shadowy path leads to a distant millhouse, all visible through the superimposed dream picture of the young man with his bride leaving the village church, changing a moment later to the daringly intimate vision of the girl in a voluminous white nightgown, the mood of longing intensified by the sombre colours, black, dusky olive-green, blue-green, and storm-charged grey, stabbed by the blinding white of the nightdress.

The magic of these double images has been preserved in tangible form in the remarkable coloured verse cards issued by Edwin Bamforth after the turn of the century. He used his father's old negatives in the production of these postcards, and though their success prompted him to make new subjects by similar methods, many of which have great charm, he was never able to use photography so imaginatively as Joseph Bamforth had done, nor to surpass his poetic interpretations of *Thora*, *Eileen Allanagh*, *Kathleen Mavourneen*, *Laddie*, *Don't Go Down the Mine*, *Dad*, and *The Newsboy's Debt*.

Never once is there any attempt in the slides made from life models, as all too often in the films which succeeded them, to dramatize the stories according to stage conventions. The composers of the slides never forgot that the projected image is two-dimensional and gives simultaneously the effect of an actual happening and, unlike the theatre, of a picture. They show us a sequence of scenes which, diverse in time and space, do not seem in the least arbitrary and are so little disturbing that we look at them as calmly as at a collection of the picture postcards, which, as we have just seen, some of them afterwards became. They fill the blank circle or rectangle of screen with images which seem significant as very few film images, apart from those of Chaplin and the early Russian producers, have done.

The plastic foreshortened form of Annie in *Ostler Joe* dying on her bed of shame, the photographed face and rounded arms untinted and of ghastly pallor against the indigo wall; Joe himself kneeling against a sagging bed, back

towards us, his ample person straining at his skin-tight clothes deeply pathetic
and yet hilariously funny; the hesitant child lifting the latch of the garden gate
in *A Peep Behind the Scenes*, the figure and the bold arabesque of the gateway
between its stone pillars standing out against a precipitous, misty Yorkshire
landscape; the woman in a flounced dress, blue-white spread across a plush and
varnished room of pink and purple in *The Garden of Roses*; crippled Nan in
Not Wanted lying unconscious in the dusty lane beside the farmcart and heavy
white horse which she has saved from collision with a pony-and-trap; the
bearded hero of *The Drunkard's Return* kneeling in prayer in his battered silk hat
in a tree-shaded sandy road beneath an apple-green evening sky; the young
girl in her blue shawl and immense flowered hat in *The Little Testament*
standing against an unbroken wall of dull green and a screen of even duller,
yellower green; the toy-like, ivy-mantled waiting-room of *The Level Crossing*
set against a background of trees as wild and mysterious as a forest by Salvator
Rosa: these and many other slides are as memorable as some of the finest
paintings and cast an even more potent spell, perhaps because they can spring
to full life only when they are cast upon the bright screen in the hushed and
darkened room.

The strong impact made by these compositions depends largely on the
design, but the unusually subtle colouring is also one of the chief sources of
their strange power. As in the case of the topographical slides described in the
last chapter, the glasses were painted by girls and women employed by the
manufacturers; the pigments used were exactly the same as those already
enumerated as serving for the colouring of hand-drawn slides, and this was
responsible for the characteristic range of plum, purple, green-yellow, lime-
green, shining turquoise, rose-pink and crimson; yet only the rarest sense of
colour could have produced the ravishing harmonies with which these life-
model slides enchant us. The white frame of a glass-house gleams in clear spring
light in a fresh green kitchen garden, rendered with the sparkle of a Sisley; a
blue latticed porch dominates a landscape of purple boulders; a scene in a bar
plays upon tones of rust, ochre brown, and green-black as tender as those in
Hogarth's 'Wanstead Assembly'; a woman in a lime-yellow dress is placed
on a plum-coloured sofa against a faded pink-sprigged wallpaper and white
transparent curtains. And not only sensibility but great skill went into the
colouring of these slides. The glass on which the painting had to be done

measures but 4¼ in. square, while the projected image extends to at least 6 ft. across; and yet not a blurred outline or inaccuracy of any kind mars the picture on the screen.

As much as anything else, of course, the impressive quality of these figure slides springs from the feeling and artistry of the actors who posed for them. These early heroes and heroines of the screen are nameless; they wear no make-up, they are not in the least glamorous, the absolute naturalness of their faces is in marked contrast to the artificial masks of the modern cinema. The casts are extraordinarily varied; it is rare for the same persons to appear in different sets of slides. A tall, dark, bearded man with a fierce eye and prominent nose takes the part of Augustus in *A Peep behind the Scenes* and is seen again as the villain of *The Gipsy's Revenge*, as the hero of *The Drunkard's Return*, and as a fisherman in *The Two Golden Lilies*. Another much younger fisherman in this last sequence also plays the character of the elder brother in *Mother's Last Words*. A large-boned, long-nosed woman features opposite the bearded man in each of the tales in which he takes a major role, doubling as the aunt and the mother of Mrs. Walton's story; she figures, too, as the drug-addict in *The Heavenly City*. An unusually talented little girl gives a finished performance as Rosalie and a most spirited interpretation of the little boy stolen by the gipsies in *The Gipsy's Revenge*. Her power of expression and control is unequalled by any of the many other gifted child players of the lantern-slide drama. In some of the sets the camera occasionally registers an unsuitable expression, such as the ill-repressed, though most endearing, giggles of the three little boys in *The Two Sovereigns* where one lies groaning with the pain of a broken leg while the other two are supposed to be looking on in sympathy. But the heroine of *A Peep behind the Scenes* is never once guilty of an awkward gesture or irrelevant emotion, despite the strain of holding each position for the long exposure necessary at that time.

Many of the most talented of these actors seem to have made but one appearance. Annie and Joe in *Ostler Joe*, two of the most unforgettable of the lantern-slide characters, are not seen again; no producer presented the clever girl and boy in *Teddy's Button* with a contract for a new slide sequence; nobody sufficiently appreciated the delicate charm of the child in *Dick's Fairy* to offer her another part; the eloquent movements of the young woman in *Jane Conquest*, the expressive face of Nan in *Not Wanted*, the brilliant miming of the

The heroine of *The Curtain* gazes into the future

The hero of *The Scent of the Lilies* thinks of his youth and his dead love

In these Victorian slides from life models two pictures are combined, a device often used to portray characters' thoughts

The vision of the ball, from *Robin Adair*

The sea breaks in on the sleepers in *What are the Wild Waves Saying?*

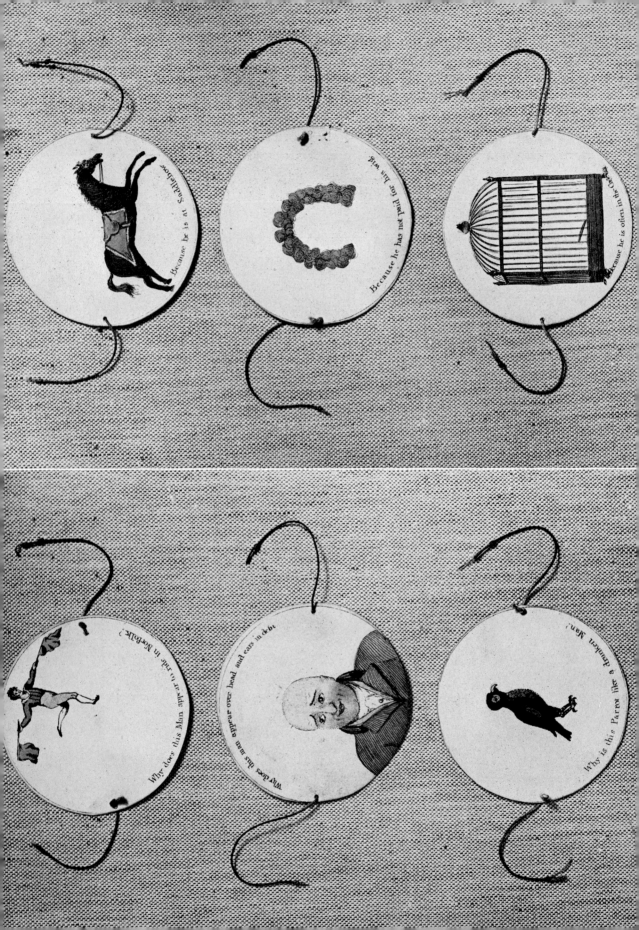

No Star System α

girl in *Curfew Shall Not Ring Tonight*, the seductive powers of the languid heroine of *Sing Me to Sleep*, all were lost to the screen after one isolated performance.

I mentioned earlier that Bamforth employed local talent for his slides. Other slide makers also worked in this way and it is therefore understandable that the actors, the veriest amateurs, should be continually changing. Although their names are not recorded, the bearded man, the long-nosed woman, and the accomplished child, who are conspicuous for their appearance in several tales, seem to have achieved that distinction by becoming professionals. For they took part in some of the first films made in England. The slides in which they are seen were all made by Bamforth, who in 1899 joined forces with another Yorkshire firm, Riley Brothers, to take up cinematography. They must have recognized the rare ability of these village players, for they at once cast them for the principal parts in the film of *The Gipsy's Revenge*, issuing this melodrama as a set of slides at the same time.

It is obvious that the makers of these life-model slides were almost always compelled to work with limited means. Robin Adair's shabby boots and Bamforth's repeated use of the same 'props' have already been noted. And even a child would realize that the historic costumes in *Mary, Queen of Scots* are mere paper and pasteboard. Poor interiors are on the whole rendered more convincingly than the homes of the rich. The nursery of the squire's children in *Three Little Wise Men* is not much more handsomely equipped than the blacksmith's cottage where the boys go to dispense charity. The wealthy uncle's bedroom in *Probable Sons* is furnished with shiny linoleum, patched wallpaper, and a rickety iron bedstead. None of these pictures has been made from an existing room; they have been contrived by means of painted back-cloths and few pieces of furniture. In one of them, the cottage parlour, a strip of grass can be glimpsed in the foreground where the length of cloth begins that does duty for the floor, and the white ceiling is the open sky. Such an arrangement was probably necessitated by the difficulty of making long exposures indoors with such a large number of people on the set in positions so far from easy and also by the fact that photographers had not yet begun to use artificial light for indoor work.

Yet, however humbly or clumsily constructed, all these settings are for us steeped in period interest. Every ornament, wallpaper, patterned hanging, every

Thaumatrope discs: one side poses the riddle, and spinning the disc by means of the strings provides the answer. (Barnes Collection)

table and chair, is charged with the atmosphere of the late Victorian era, an atmosphere more strongly felt, oddly enough, than when, as occasionally happens, the background has been photographed from an actual scene, interesting though it may be to ascertain the precise date of *Not Wanted* from a sale notice of 1891 on the taproom wall, and to remark that the country mansions in *Probable Sons* and *Three Little Wise Men* are precisely of their period: the turreted, gabled, Gothic-Moorish confections of the 1880's.

Very often, owing to lack of resources, the narrative is visualized with fewer slides than would make it completely intelligible without the read or recited text. But to a modern viewer the fragmentary, enigmatical character of some of the sets increases their fascination. One of the most evocative of all the sequences I have seen consists of some fifty numbered slides for which the title *The Bronze Statue* survives, but for which no accompanying written matter has so far come to light.

The first scene shows a sea-shore with rocky cliffs, wilder than anything found in nature, where the realistic equestrian statue of a French cavalry officer of about 1870 confronts the waves. A group of people, including the comic figure of a man in an over-long frock-coat and concertina trousers and two little girls, are standing with their backs towards us gazing at the monument. Next, the same scene in the grip of a fearful storm is flashed on to the screen. A ship is on the point of sinking just as a lifeboat draws near. The statue is conspicuously absent from this picture, so it is natural to suppose that it commemorates some act of heroism on this disastrous night. The two girls of the first slide are immediately afterwards seen in earnest conversation together beside the bronze horseman.

A moment later we are shown the same girls in bed in one of those scantily furnished attics so dear to the slide makers. Some years have passed, for the children have grown to be about fourteen years of age. Savage rain can be seen beating down outside and the hands of a clock opposite the bed point to midnight. One of the girls starts up, puts on a cloak with a frilled hood, stealthily leaves the house, and goes down to the shore as though in conformance to some vow made earlier. The rain lashes the choppy water and a gale blows back the girl's cloak (kept in position during the long exposure by a thread which has not been entirely spotted out) as she stands with arms outstretched towards the monument. The rider responds by slowly lowering the arm in which he is brandishing a sabre and as slowly dismounting. The heroine shrinks back and, just before the statue touches her, summons the strength to turn and run for home. The expression of terror on her plain little face as she regains her door is as impressive as the perfection of the composition of the cloaked form against the plain wall of the house.

Next morning wind and rain have yielded to a radiant sky and a gentle sea and the events of the night might seem a dream but for the alarming fact that the bronze figure has vanished from his horse; a crowd stares at the empty saddle.

In the following picture the girl has become a woman. One day, by chance, to judge from her look of surprise, she meets a fair young man at a street corner who is dressed precisely like the statue. They sit together in an ivied bower high above the little town, but the young woman turns away from the attractive youth. Then, in the depths of a moonless night, the horseman is seen to remount his bronze steed. As he regains the saddle, his upraised arm stiffens into position. It is as though he had never been quickened into life. The heroine is again sitting among the ivy, this time fervently clasping the hands of a young man uncannily like the first.

Are they one and the same? And did the girl's unholy infatuation for the statue keep her from her true love on the first occasion? Was the original of the statue still living and did he send his bronze counterpart, endowed with movement by the powers of evil, back to his sculptured mount when the girl had proved her strength to resist his sinister charms?

We may never know. It is all utterly mysterious, ambiguous, and uncertain, but it exemplifies a truth often forgotten by the makers of films, that full explanatory detail is not only unnecessary but obstructive to the creation of a world of purely visual poetry.

8

The Persistence of Vision

A moving mouse is more engrossing to the attention than a roomful
of precious things.

D. S. MCCOLL

THOUGH all the categories and effects of the film were anticipated by the
forms of pictorial entertainment described in the foregoing chapters, and
although many of the illusions of movement achieved by the clever showmen
of past centuries were remarkably convincing, neither the panoramas nor
dioramas, nor the play of shadows, nor any of the images projected by mirrors
or lanterns, not even when living models had posed for them, were true moving
pictures. The invention by means of which human beings were to be shown in
full, spontaneous action instead of in a series of stills animated by means of
dissolvers and trick glasses, owed nothing to any of the popular entertainments
to which, on a cultural level, the cinema was the successor and counterpart.
It was the result of experiment throughout the nineteenth century with a
variety of scientific toys based on the phenomenon of the 'persistence of
vision'—the physiological idiosyncrasy that the retina of the eye retains the
impression of an object for a fraction of a second after its disappearance.

The phenomenon had been noticed many centuries before it was practically
applied. Lucretius mentions the fact of persistence of vision, though only in
connection with images seen in a dream; Ptolemy, in his treatise on optics,
describes a disc, one section of which is coloured, and declares that if it is
rapidly revolved the whole will be of that colour. The twelfth-century Arabian
philosopher, Alhazen, who was also interested in perspective boxes like those

121

evolved by Alberti, refers to persistence of vision, and Leonardo gives an account of it. But until the first quarter of the nineteenth century, when the popular imagination was more and more dominated by the fantasy of the picture that moved, very little attempt was made to demonstrate the principle.

At the very beginning of this period the London Stereoscopic Company brought out a toy which showed that the same object could be exhibited in more than one place at once by means of this same phenomenon of persistence of vision. A piece of wire bent to the outline of one side of some such symmetrical figure as a vase, for instance, was set in a hollow, vertical, metal spindle. When this was revolved the figure appeared complete. The same toy was also manufactured in France under the name 'la Toupie éblouissante'.

In 1825 a further step was taken when Dr. John Ayrton Paris, who was born at Cambridge and practised medicine at Penzance, proved that it was possible to exhibit two different objects in the same place at the same time. He invented a pretty little contrivance to which he gave the evocative name of the 'Thaumatrope'. He had already described the principle of this toy in a work called *Philosophy in Sport made Science in Earnest; being an Attempt to Illustrate the First Principles of Natural Philosophy by the Aid of Popular Toys and Sports*, the prototype of those books for the young combining instruction with pleasure which were in increasing demand throughout the Victorian period. The Thaumatrope was published by William Phillips of George Yard, Lombard Street, on April 2nd of the year of its invention. It consisted of a little round box labelled '*Thaumatropical Amusement*', containing a number of delicate paper discs each with strings attached on either side so that it might be twirled between fingers and thumbs. Each face of the disc presented a different image, but as soon as it was rotated both images merged together. A bare tree put on leaves, a bald man acquired a wig, a parrot entered a cage, a rider mounted his horse. The wirily outlined devices, hand-coloured in clear reds, yellows, greens, and blues, were accompanied by absurd mottoes and riddles. 'Why is this Parrot like a drunken Man?' ran the legend beneath the bird. 'Because he is often in the Cage', came the answer on the reverse of the roundel. Below the figure of the rider was printed the poser: 'Why does this Man appear to ride in Norfolk?' the answer to which, on the side showing the spirited black horse, read: 'Because he is at Saddlebow.' On one side of another card was depicted a watchman and on the other his box. When the card was twirled the watchman seemed to be comfortably asleep at his post. The accompanying epigram was as follows:

'The caprice of this watchman surpasses all bounds;
He ne'er sits in his box but when going his rounds;
While he no sooner rests—'tis a strange paradox—
Than he flies from his post, and turns out of his box.'

The inventor's address to the public, printed inside the lid of the box, ended thus:

'The inventor confidently anticipates the favour and patronage of an enlightened and liberal public on the well grounded assurance that "one good turn deserves another", and he trusts that his discovery may afford the happy means of giving activity to wit that has long been stationary, of revolutionizing the present system of standing jokes, and of putting into rapid circulation the most approved *bon-mots*.'

The images produced by the Thaumatrope can be made to vary according to the degree of tension applied to the strings. If these are suddenly tightened while the card is still in motion the rider, for instance, seems to turn a somersault over the head of his steed, while on relaxing the strings he will again sit in the saddle.

Dr. Paris's toy was sold at the Royal Institution in Albemarle Street for seven shillings and sixpence. The powerful attraction of the idea of a moving picture could scarcely be more vividly demonstrated than by the fact that it enticed this august establishment to enter the field of commerce. It was an idea which was in the air at that time. Throughout the history of the mechanical development of the animated image the same inventions were continually being produced by different people almost simultaneously. Visitors to the Science Museum in South Kensington will find the invention of the Thaumatrope attributed to Sir John Herschel. And this eminent philosopher did indeed illustrate the principle of the toy in the same year that Paris patented his discs.

In his *Passages from the Life of a Philosopher* Charles Babbage describes how one night after dinner Herschel showed him a method of seeing both sides of a shilling at once by spinning it on the table. Babbage happened to mention this on the following day to his friend Dr. Fritton, who a short time afterwards brought him a charming illustration of the principle in the shape of a roundel of card suspended between two pieces of sewing silk. Upon one side of the card was drawn a rat, on the other a trap. Babbage also relates that after Paris's Thaumatrope came out another example appeared which enjoyed great popularity among the members of the Royal Society. On one side of the disc was represented a Thaumatrope (the design on it being a penny piece) with the motto: 'How to turn a penny.' On the reverse was drawn a gentleman in black holding out his hands in the act of spinning a Thaumatrope, the motto reading: 'A New Trick from Paris.'

Further advance in the creation of illusory movement was made possible by Dr. Roget's discovery, also in 1825, that the spokes of a rotating wheel were apparently stationary when seen through a series of vertical slots. Shortly afterwards, by means of an apparatus known as Faraday's Wheel, Faraday demonstrated that when two cogged wheels with an equal number of teeth revolve at equal speed in opposite directions, one in front of the other, the eye perceives a stationary image of one wheel only. Owing to the persistence of vision of the eye the strong impression made each time the cogs of the two wheels coincide is retained by the retina, while the weaker picture formed when the cogs of one wheel passes over the spaces of the other fails to register. Faraday also astonished his colleagues by proving that if a transparent, brightly illuminated star was placed behind a cardboard disc with a single narrow opening extending from the circumference to the centre, the whole of the star except the part immediately opposite the opening would be hidden, but that if the disc were rotated at high speed the whole of the star would become visible.

Faraday demonstrated his wheel to the Fellows of the Royal Society in 1831, but before that date, in 1828, a Belgian philosopher and scientist, Joseph Antoine Ferdinand Plateau, had made exactly the same discovery. In 1836 he invented an instrument called the Anorthoscope, which reversed the illusion observed by Roget and produced a correct image from a distorted original. But before this, in 1830, he patented a contrivance which combined the principle illustrated by the Thaumatrope with Roget's, Faraday's, and his

Zoetrope bands and Phenakistiscope discs. (Barnes Collection)

Replica of the Rudge Lantern Slide Projector, invented *c.* 1875 by J. A. R. Rudge, one of the earliest instruments devised to produce an illusion of movement from a series of photographs projected on to the lantern screen. (Science Museum, London)

The Projecting Phenakistiscope, an example of *c.* 1890 made in Germany. (Barnes Collection)

An early experiment in photographing movement by Eadward Muybridge, *c.* 1883. He used forty cameras, a Dallmeyer lens, and an electro-magnetic shutter

own experiments with rotating wheels, spokes, and cogs. This invention, the Phenakistiscope, was the progenitor of all the later and more complicated forms of motion pictures.

Just as in the case of the Thaumatrope, the idea, engendered by the climate of the age, occurred almost simultaneously to another mind. Only one month later, when no description of Plateau's Phenakistiscope had yet been published, S. Stampfer of Vienna brought out exactly the same toy under the name of the Stroboscope.

Plateau is one of the most remarkable figures in the history of living pictures, a direct contrast in his single-minded devotion to science to the showmen-inventors of the previous chapters. Born in 1801, he devoted himself from boyhood to the study of optics, especially in their physiological aspect. At the age of twenty-eight, while experimenting with the effect of light on the retina, he exposed his eyes for considerable time to the full blaze of the sun. He was blinded, but partially recovered after some months of agony. It was during the ensuing period of half-sight that Plateau invented the Phenakistiscope and was appointed Professor of Physics at Ghent. But by 1843 he was totally blind. Despite this terrible handicap he continued his experiments and inventions with the aid of a devoted wife who carried out all his instructions. He died at the age of eighty-three, still in harness. There is something strangely moving in the thought of this noble man, who would doubtless have been horrified by many aspects of the cinema, contributing so largely to the development of a popular entertainment, the enjoyment of which depends wholly on the sense of which he was himself deprived.

The English equivalent of the Phenakistiscope, brought out by T. Baynes, was variously called the Fantascope, Phantascope, Phantasmascope, Magic Disc, Kaleidorama, or McLean's Optical Illusions or Magic Panorama. The toy is constructed as follows: The edge of a large pasteboard disc is deeply notched to form cogs between each of which are painted figures in a number of positions. By means of nut and screw the disc is attached to a spindle and rapidly revolved in front of a mirror. The image in the looking-glass performs a series of convincing movements, graceful or grotesque according to the drawing. A dancer pirouettes, a frog leaps over a rat, a devil turns somersaults while a horseman gallops round and round him has hard as he can go, a swallow darts about a rose bush, a cat chases a sparrow, a lady and gentleman waltz, fantastic ogre heads approach the centre of the disc, growing larger and larger, then suddenly recede.

A Phenakistiscope roundel owned by John and William Barnes is decorated with the exaggerated features of a human face in such a way that as it revolves the mirror flings back a preposterous animated image of enormous bespectacled eyes shifting rapidly from side to side, while a prim mouth opens to swallow an endless procession of rats. This and other discs for the Phenakistiscope were issued by the Holborn firm of Clarke, well known earlier in the century as publishers of the Juvenile Drama.

It was the Phenakistiscope which prompted the first attempts at the projection of a continually moving image, for the toy was in such demand that it became urgently necessary to accommodate a number of viewers instead of only one. Plateau himself attacked the problem in 1849. He place sixteen images in progressive series round the margin of a glass disc, and in front of this, in reverse direction and at a speed four times as great, revolved an opaque disc with four slots. All parts of the disc except that showing the erect image were screened off. The front of the apparatus could be observed by many people at the same time. Plateau's design represented a devil blowing up a fire and it produced so striking a sensation that the inventor was encouraged to use photographic instead of drawn pictures. In 1852 he secured a series of posed photographs of a workman using a pestle and mortar. The results, when these photographs were combined by means of the Phenakistiscope, showed how impossible it was to obtain a naturalistic effect of movement from a number of posed attitudes. The workman, when he was allowed to see the moving image, cried out, 'But that's not how I work!'

Plateau's apparatus could easily have been made practicable for projection, but he does not seem to have suggested this. And the first attempt to project the differently speeded discs was made by the Austrian lieutenant Franz Uchatius in 1851. He found that he could not show figures more than 6 in. high; and in 1853 he invented a most ingenious contraption which he demonstrated at the Vienna Academy of Sciences and which was manufactured by the Viennese optical house of Prokesch (later Fritsch). The images were painted on the margin of a transparent disc which remained stationary. A lens was placed in front of each image, the whole circle of lenses being capable of adjustment in order that all the optic axes should cross at the place where the picture was formed on the screen. The separate lenses then all threw their respective images in the same place, the succession of the series being achieved by means of a revolving limelight behind the pictures, only one of which was lit at a time. Thus the source of light was the only thing that moved. Uchatius called his invention the Lantern Wheel of Light.

Much later in the century there appeared a device known as the Ross Wheel of Life designed for use with the lantern. The disc bearing the figures was slowly revolved. One sector was removed from the opaque disc, which rotated once while the transparent disc moved one stage.

Meanwhile in 1869 A. B. Brown had patented a form of Projecting Phenakistiscope in the United States which incorporated a mechanical contrivance essential to the invention of cinematography, a Maltese cross arrangement and a shutter. The former ensures the production of intermittent movement: jerking a picture into the path of the projector so that it can be flung on a screen; holding it there very briefly, then jerking it aside again and at the same time putting the next picture into position for projection. The shutter is the means by which the picture is hidden during the small fraction of a second when it is being moved on and off the screen. By means of the single-blade shutter and Maltese cross device of the hand-operated Projecting Phenakistiscope, the smoothly moving painted figures of blacksmiths working at an anvil, negro boys diving into a lake, horses jumping over a hurdle, urchins sliding on a pond or pole-vaulting, appeared in full movement and almost life-size upon the screen.

In 1834, two years after the appearance of the Phenakistiscope, W. G. Horner of Bristol, who has already been encountered in these pages as the owner of the Regent's Park Coliseum and the inventor of ingenious diorama effects, produced a toy which he called the Daedelum or Wheel of Life. It does not, however, seem to have been put on the market until 1867, and ten years after that date Robert Routledge still referred to it as one of the most recently fabricated of toys based on the principle of the persistence of vision. In 1860, more than twenty years after Horner had published a description of his apparatus in the *Philosophical Magazine,* A Frenchman, Désvignes, patented a daedelum, though without giving it a name. And in 1867 the selfsame contrivance was brought out in the United States by William E. Lincoln of Providence under the name of Zoetrope, by which it became generally known.

The Zoetrope consists of a thin, slot-pierced metal drum capable of revolving easily and readily about its axis by turning horizontally on a pivot in the heavy base on which it stands. An example in the Barnes Collection made by the London Stereoscopic and Photographic Company in about 1868 has an elegantly chased base and an olive-green drum painted white inside. It seems to be the very counterpart of an instrument which George R. Sims admired in the window of the Stereoscopic Company in Cheapside in 1869, and of another which delighted Baudelaire as a child with its figures of precisely moving dancers and jugglers.

Each Zoetrope is accompanied by a set of paper strips equal in length to the circumference of the drum and in width to half its depth, and picturing in flat colours and simple outline figures in the various stages of a movement, such as skipping, leaping, dancing, or tossing balls, the number of figures on a single strip corresponding to the number of slots in the drum. When one of these strips is placed inside the drum and the figures are viewed through the slot while the instrument is rotated, they leap into vivid action: a negro jumps through a hoop, a juggler throws his balls vigorously into the air, a dolphin undulates through heaving billows, while a seagull skims the water with steady wing-beats.

The movement exhibited by the Zoetrope is jerky in character, and for this reason the rather abrupt gestures made by people or creatures in the act of leaping, dancing, swimming, falling, or fighting are more generally chosen for representation. The effect on the eye is so dazzling that it is impossible to look through the slots for more than a minute or two at a time. In the Praxinoscope, constructed by Emile Reynaud and patented in Paris on August 30th, 1877, and in England on November 13th of the same year, this disadvantage has been very cleverly overcome by abolishing the slots and placing mirrors in the centre of the drum to reflect and animate the circling images.

Reynaud improved even on this by devising the most enchanting of all these toys, the Praxinoscope Theatre. Here the tiny figures move as if on a stage with a glass-fronted proscenium. A juggler tosses four balls into the air and at the same time balances a drum on the end of a stick resting on his nose; a child in an ample bathing costume swims with regular strokes in an orna-mental lake in a formal garden with a French château in the background; the scene changes to winter and three small boys skate on the frozen lake or play at leapfrog, running in turn down a flight of steps.

The mechanism of this delightful toy was based on two drums, one within the other. The long strips of paper on which were printed the phases of each movement were placed inside the outer drum, and round the inner drum were fixed a series of small rectangular pieces of glass. When the characters were revolved in the drum their flying images were reflected in the centre drum. Between the viewpoint through the proscenium and the turn-table with the drums another section was fixed which also had a rectangular opening, and into small grooves in this frame little pieces of scenery were placed, printed and coloured in much the same tradition as the Toy Theatre sheets produced at Épinal. The effect of this was that while the spectator saw the figures in full movement, the scenery remained perfectly still.

Reynaud experimented further and soon invented his Projected Praxinoscope, which cast upon the screen a complete variety performance of jugglers, acrobats, and dancers.

Another toy based on the Zoetrope and making an impression similar to that of the Praxinoscope Theatre, though using an entirely different arrangement to create the illusion of movement, was the Viviscope, invented in 1890. With this instrument an endless paper band with figures drawn on it is placed on the outside of the cylinder, which is interrupted by an opening designed as a miniature proscenium with classical pillars. The band is in continual contact with the cylinder except where two small vertical rollers are interposed. As long as it is in contact with the cylinder the band remains stationary, but the rollers travel round behind it (set in motion by a hand attached to the base of the Viviscope) and as they press the band outwards and then return it to contact with the cylinder they push it round, its advance being equal to the width of one picture.

Yet another variation on the Zoetrope was the Tachyscope, made by a German, Ottomar Anschütz, in 1887. Except that it had a much wider cylinder to accommodate a greater number of pictures, it was constructed on exactly the same principles as the Zoetrope, but Anchütz advanced a step nearer to the discovery of cinematography by making use of photography. He reproduced the movements of a horse and rider leaping over a hurdle from a series of photographs.

Ottomar Anschütz was one of the pioneers in the taking of instantaneous photographs. Those he used for his Tachyscope were taken in 1885. It remained only to combine the moving photographic image with the principles of projection embodied by the Projecting Phenakistiscope for cinematography to come into existence.

As early as 1875 a projector had been made which created an illusion of motion smoother and closer to that contrived by the cinematograph than anything so far seen. It was named the Rudge Projector after its inventor, J. A. Rudge. This device relied on an intermittent mechanism which was basically the same as that employed by Brown for this Projecting Phenakistiscope. It successfully applied principles which Sir Charles Wheatstone, the inventor of the stereoscope, had attempted, with poor results, to incorporate in a viewing apparatus more than thirty years earlier.

Rudge's lantern comprised a cylindrical lamp-house fitted with a revolving gallery which held seven lantern slides. The slides were photographic, each prepared from a separate negative made from carefully posed figures. For Rudge's aim was to show a photographic image completing a movement smoothly and naturalistically instead of projecting, as Brown had done, a drawn and coloured picture, the movement of which could have been equally well achieved by means of a slipping slide. The photographs were projected in swift succession by the turning of a handle connected to a shaft carrying at its far end a tongue or pin which engaged with a forked slot at the junction of each pair of slides, so that, as the shaft turned, the pin moved the gallery round to the extent of one picture and locked it into position. The brief period when the slides were in motion was masked by a scissor-shaped shutter operated by a cam on the front end of the shaft to which were fixed two blades of ground glass. The posed photographs were, of course, no more successful in simulating the movements of a living being than Plateau's pictures of the workman had been, though Rudge had cunningly chosen to represent a wholly unnatural action: that of a man removing his own head and replacing it.

It was the study of this instrument which enabled Friese-Greene to produce in 1899 the first practical camera and projector for use with a perforated celluloid band.

The first suggestion of how actually to photograph a moving object or creature did not come from Anschütz but from a Frenchman, Du Mont. He designed an apparatus as far back as 1861 in which a shutter was geared to expose the plates when they were perpendicular to the axis of the lens. The sensitive surfaces succeeded one another at regular intervals, being placed either on a prismatic drum or sliding frame, or else dropped in turn from an upper chamber into a lower one. Three years later Duclos du Hauron filed an application for a patent for an 'apparatus designed to reproduce by photography any scenes, with all the transformations undergone during a predetermined time'.

In 1870 Marey, a French physiologist, began his extensive analyses of the motion of birds, greatly advanced in his work by the continual efforts made at that time to increase the sensibility of photo-surfaces. In 1872 Eadward Muybridge, an Englishman who spent most of his life in America, and whose real name was James Edward Muggeridge, also began to experiment with the object of discovering the successive attitudes which collectively made up a given movement. Marey confined himself to the method of casting his series of momentary exposures on one plate by means of a single lens, but Muybridge's plan was to take successive views of a human being or animal passing in front of a series of cameras. In 1877 he took a sequence of photographs to prove that all four feet of a horse were off the ground at certain moments. His pictures were little more than silhouettes with the minimum definition, but they accomplished Muybridge's chief aim: to capture the various attitudes of a horse; and he obtained a patent for his method in 1897. He used between ten and thirty cameras, the shutters of which were released in turn by strings which were attached to the cameras and pulled down by the animals in their course.

Between 1883 and 1884 Muybridge began using forty cameras, a Dallmeyer lens, and an electro-magnetic shutter to take photographs of men and horses. In 1885 he took pictures of various animals in the Zoological Gardens of Philadelphia and in the following year he concentrated on the study of children, men, and women walking and running, of athletics, and of soldiers on the march. Some of these are reproduced in his books: *Locomotion* (1887), *Animals in Motion* (1891), and *The Human Figure in Motion* (1901). Some years before the publication of these works, in 1880, an interesting notice had appeared in *Cassell's Magazine*:

'Readers may remember that a good deal of interest was excited here and elsewhere not very long ago, by the publication of photographs and engravings illustrating the various motions of a trotting horse. Since these instantaneous photographs were taken, an instrument called the Zoogyroscope has been invented for the purpose of imparting something of a lifelike character to the pictorial representation in question. Mr. Muybridge, the inventor, describes it as a circular glass bearing a series of photographs of the animal to be represented in motion. As the glass is turned, the photographs, which are successively illuminated by an oxy-hydrogen lantern, throw upon the screen a single, continuous, yet ever-changing picture, which is considered to be so admirable an imitation of the "real-live" horse, that nothing but the clatter of the hoofs and the breath of the nostrils is wanted to render the delusion complete. The Zoogyroscope can, it is scarcely necessary to add, be applied to photographs of other animals beside the horse.'

Muybridge's projector, which clearly had something in common with that of Rudge and with the Projecting Phenakistiscope, was provided with a slotted metal disc in front. The disc and the picture plate were revolved in opposite directions by turning a handle and the result was a projection on the screen of a series of moving images.

The inventive Muybridge was not satisfied with the photography and projection of movement. In 1883 he discussed with Edison the possibility of using his Zoogyroscope in conjunction with the phonograph 'so as to combine and reproduce simultaneously, in the presence of an audience, visible actions and audible words'. Some years after the appearance of the Zoogyroscope, Edison produced the Kinetoscope, in which the perforated film was first used which was so largely responsible for the rapid progress of effective projection. But news of Edison's invention did not reach England until 1891, when a meagre account of it was given in *The Times*. And the first public exhibition of his instrument at the Brooklyn Institute took place only in 1893, while it was not shown in England until a year later. Long before this, in June 1889, W. Friese-Green and M. Evans patented the first really practical machine capable of securing a record of any event and suitable for the subsequent reproduction of moving pictures of past occurrences. Muybridge's glass disc was replaced by the celluloid ribbon and three hundred exposures could be made at the rate of ten in each second. Only two months afterwards, in August 1889, Messrs. Donisthorne and Crofts also produced an apparatus for successfully projecting the celluloid ribbon.

Of these instruments, the Kinetoscope was the only one of a remotely popular nature, and there had so far been no projected living picture which could be called a great public success. Edison's first pictures were microscopic, which rendered them quite useless for exhibition to a large audience, and he failed to devise a satisfactory method of enlarging his images. The mechanical details of his perfected Kinetoscope were, however, unique, and provided the basis for the machine patented by the Brothers Lumière in the spring of 1895 and used in the first cinematograph theatre in the world. The Cinématographe Lumière Frères was opened on December 28th in the cellar of the Grand Café in the boulevard des Capucins, Paris. By 1896 H. Goodwin Norton was using a film projector in combination with his magic lantern to vary his lantern entertainments. These very early films were simple pictures of trains, soldiers marching, and waves breaking; one of those exhibited in the Grand Café consisted merely of a stream of workers coming out of the factory of the Brothers Lumière.

Such factual records were soon subordinated to pictures exploiting the possibilities of the film as a medium for fabulous, fantastic spectacles in the tradition of its visual forerunners, the Diorama, the shadow play, and the magic-lantern show, and even when they claimed to offer their public straightforward reportage, producers were inclined to concentrate on calamity and to pile on the horror. An appalling disaster at sea was shown in full detail in 1912 as an interlude in a music-hall show, while the audience sang 'Rocked in the Cradle of the Deep' to the tinkle of a piano. The crude pathos which had stirred the humble audiences of the life-model lantern displays was an indispensable ingredient of the films which took their place. The story of *A Rogue's Redemption*, shown in about 1906, illustrates the close connection in this respect between the two forms of picture sequences:

A woman, the mother of a little girl, hides an escaped convict from the pursuing warders. Some time later he breaks into a house. In the room in which he finds himself a child is lying asleep in a cot and he discovers that she is the daughter of the woman to whom he owes his freedom. The child awakens and is terrified by the sight of the strange man. But the burglar gently soothes her and she falls asleep again clutching one of his fingers. He prefers to risk detection rather than startle her anew and he is still there when the mother enters. Once again she helps him and in the final scene he is making an honest living in a workshop.

The inventors who had made the true photographic moving picture a reality had been interested in its mechanics rather than its matter. But now that it was established as a form of entertainment it attracted to itself the same type of showman as those who had been involved with all the earlier forms of animated pictures. Meliès, who exhibited his astonishing films with the aid of the Edison Kinetoscope, began his career as a famous illusionist and conjurer, and the first American film makers had served their apprenticeship as the owners of booths where the public wondered at spectacles and illusions of every kind.

The great popular invention of the cinema was the culmination of centuries of effort to impart lifelike movement to a two-dimensional picture. It also gave rise to a private diversion, of very minor importance, it is true, yet of interest in any account of the history of living pictures because it combines the moving photographic image with the idea of the peepshow. Small prints were made from the cinematograph films and these were bound up into fat little books called Mutoscopes and sprang to life when they were flicked over by hand or by some mechanical device. A clever contrivance of this kind, called the Filoscope, was patented by Short in 1898. Successive cinematograph pictures are mounted one behind another in their correct order upon a metal lever. When this lever is pressed downwards the images are sharply released in turn from a projection on the framework which interrupts their free path, and a lifelike appearance of motion is produced.

Another, truly magical, form of animated peepshow was the Kinora, which appeared in 1897. A handsome instrument in the Barnes Collection is fitted with three lenses so that three persons can view the spectacle simultaneously. The pictures are operated by a clockwork motor which is wound up by a large knob protruding from one side of the machine and started or stopped by a smaller adjacent control. Situated at the top of the instrument, as in some of the peepshows described earlier, is a mirrored flap which ensures that adequate light is reflected for the subjects to be seen with the utmost distinction. The whole is mounted on a metal column hinged at the top to allow the Kinora to be placed at a suitable angle for viewing. The body of the apparatus is of wood, stained black, with an ornate proscenium of scrollwork enveloping the lenses in a gentle curve. The foot of the column is attached to a wooden base heavily weighted to prevent tipping.

When the three viewers peep through the lenses they first of all see a little girl sitting in her bath washing her doll; this gives way to a conjurer behind a table. He picks up a bottle, pours himself a drink, throws the glass away, shows his empty hands, takes a white plate from the table and tosses it into the air. It floats across the room, assumes the position of a head on a manikin body, and begins to dance. The plate then turns into a real head and continues to dance until the conjurer makes it vanish into thin air by striking it with the bottle. Next two children hurl pillows at each other and this is followed by a scene in Trafalgar Square with horse-drawn traffic and a throng of pedestrians, and then by a glimpse of an American fairground with a huge switchback and two car-loads of gesticulating, open-mouthed passengers.

Versions of the Mutoscope-Peepshow still feature among the pier amusements of some seaside resorts. The viewer peers through an eye-piece as the pictures move to the turn of a handle, the movement of which is released by the insertion of a penny. He is rewarded with the sight of a bandit holding up a train, or a brisk stand-up fight between a shirt-sleeved hero and a bearded villain, while a lady in a picture hat and tea-gown wrings her hands energetically in the background. Though less poetic than the toy-like figures which come to jerky life on the stage of the Praxinoscope Theatre, the small scale of the moving picture exhibited by the Mutoscope and the Kinora has an irresistible charm.

The Mutoscope may still be said to play a very insignificant part in the world of entertainment, but nearly all the spectacles and toys which preceded the cinema have been forgotten except by a few enthusiasts. The pleasure of seeking out the survivors, of exploring the lumber-rooms of history, where alone some record of them may be found, of calling to life the marvellous visions, shadows, and projections which entranced long-vanished audiences, has been a sufficient delight in itself. It has also been as instructive as any of the earnest contrivers of Victorian pastimes would wish. For it places the cinema in its true perspective as but another expression of the homely popular fantasy for pictures that move which has always existed. It derives something from each of its predecessors, it even preserves the flavour of its ritual origin in the promotion of its shadow performers to the ranks of the immortal stars.

Yet the film is no more the final manifestation of man's perennial interest in the living picture than were the Phantasmagoria, the Eidophusikon, or the Panorama. Unlike the arts of drama and painting, the basic materials of which may be enriched but do not fundamentally alter, the moving picture has neither texture nor substance and is shaped by developments in technology and mechanical invention. The form it takes is therefore destined to continual change. Already the cinema is yielding to television as a mode of universal entertainment and the time may well come when the luxurious glittering picture palaces which are now an accepted feature of all our towns will be as rare as the Diorama in Regent's Park.

Bibliography

Bapst, Germain: *Essai sur l'histoire des Panoramas*, 1891

Barnes, John: Brochure for the Barnes Museum of Cinematography, St. Ives, 1963

Boehn, Max von: *Dolls and Puppets*, 1925

Born, Dr. Wolfgang: 'Peepshows of the Renaissance', *Connoisseur*, February and April, 1941

Boys' Book of Science: 1835

Brewster, Sir David: *Letters on Natural Magic*, 1833

Brown, J. H.: *Spectropia, or, Surprising Spectral Illusions*, 1864

Cellini, Benvenuto: *Memoirs*, trs. by J. A. Symonds, 1888

Gautier, Théophile: *Constantinople*, 1894 (Chapter XIV, Karagheus)

Gernsheim, Helmut: *History of the Diorama and Daguerreotype*, 1956

Groom, Edward: *The Art of Transparent Painting on Glass*, 1858

Hepworth, T. C.: *The Book of the Lantern*, 1890

Hone, William: *Ancient Mysteries Described*, 1823

Hopwood, J.: *Living Pictures*, 1915

Horner's Lantern Readings (no date)

Jacob, Georg: *Das Orientalische Schattentheater*, 1931

Jacob, Georg: *Das türkische Schattentheater*, 1900

Jacob, Georg: *Geschichte des Schattentheaters*, 1925

Jacob, Georg: *Karagöz, Komedian*, 1899

Jeanne, Paul: *Les Théâtres d'Ombres à Montmartre de 1877 à 1923* (no date)

Lardner, Dionysius: *Natural Philosophy for Schools*, 1865

Littman, Enno: *Arabische Schattenspiele*, 1901

Matthews, Brander: 'The Forerunner of the Movies', *Century Magazine*, April 1914

Mayhew, Henry: *London Labour and the London Poor*, Vol. 3, 1851

Moholy, Lucia: *A Hundred Years of Photography*, 1939

Moreck, Curt: *Sittengeschichte des Kinos* (no date)

Morley, Henry: *Memoirs of Bartholomew Fari,*1857

Norton, H. Goodwin: *The Lantern and How to Use it*, 1895

Paris, John Ayrton: *Philosophical Sport made Science in Earnest*, 1827

Parke, W. D.: *Musical Memoirs*, 1830

Pepper, John Henry: *The Boys' Playbook of Science*, 1912

Ritter, Hellmut: *Karagöz, Türkische Schattenspiele*, 1941

Sherson, Eroll: *London's Lost Theatres of the Nineteenth Century*, 1925

Sims, George R.: *Ballads and Poems*, 1885

Sims, George R.: *My Life*, 1916

Speaight, George: *History of the English Puppet Theatre*, 1955

Stenger, Erich: *Daguerre's Diorama in Berlin*, 1925

Sugavusgil, Sabri Esat: *Karagöz*, 1955

Whanislaw, H.: *Shadow Play*, 1950

Wimsatt, G.: *Chinese Shadow Shows*, 1936

The Barnes brothers have compiled a nine-volume catalogue of their great collection at St. Ives, but it has not been published yet.

There are museums of the history of the cinema in Paris and Turin.

Index

A

Abbey, J. R., collection of, 46
Acikgöz, 64
Alberti, 24, 122
Ambroise, 69, 71
Anschütz, Ottomar, 129
Astley, Philip, 69, 71
Audinot, N. M., 70
Auriol, Georges, 73

B

Bacon, Friar, 14
Bakewell, Frederick, 36
Balzac, 32
Bamforth, Edwin, 113, 114
Bamforth, J., 102-3, 105, 109, 113, 117
Barker, Henry Aston, 35, 46
Barker, Robert, 32-3, 35
Barnes Collection, 13, 27, 46, 83, 85, 87, 94, 126, 128, 139
Barton, William, 33
Beard's Eclipse, 95

Beaumont, Sir George, 34
Blès, Numa, 77
Bonnaud, Dominique, 77
Bourgeois, Constant, 34
Bouton, C. M., 36, 39, 46
Bradon, Miss, 106
Braville, 69
Brewster, Sir David, 13-14, 20
Breysig, 33
Broken Bridge, The, 69-70, 78
Brunner, 77
Burford, Robert, 35
Burton, Decimus, 35

C

Camera obscura, 23-4, 28, 29, 41
Caran d'Ache, 74
Cellini, Benvenuto, 15-18, 19, 57
Charidimos, C., 64
Charidimos, Y., 64
Chat Noir, Le, 72-5
Chaucer, 15
Chromatrope, 88

Chromolithography, 90
Constable, John, 34–5, 37–8
Cruikshank, G., 90

D

Daguerre, J. M., 36–42, 46
Davey, James, 45
David, J. L., 34
Diaphanorama, 71
Dickens, 27, 104
Diorama, 28, 36–46, 74, 97, 133
Diosse, 40
Dissolvers, 96, 97
Dunscombe, 103, 113

E

Eden, Fanny, 104
Edison, 132, 133
Eidophusikon, 29–31, 69
Eidotrope, 88
Endor, Witch of, 14
Engelbrecht brothers, 26
Eudel, Père, 71

F

Faraday, 124
Farjeon, Eleanor, 88
Filoscope, 134
Fleischer, Chev. P., 45
Fragerolle, Georges, 74, 75
Friese-Green, 130, 132

G

Gainsborough, 30–1

Galantee Show, 81–3
Garrick, 29
Geiger, Wilhelm, 56
Girodet, 43
Goethe, 71–2
Goodwin Norton, C., 96, 98, 101, 133
Gropius, Carl Wilhelm, 42–3, 46

H

Hagemann, Carl, 57
Hand shadows, 47, 89
Hearn, Lafcadio, 51, 57
Herring, Paul, 78
Herschel, Sir John, 123, 124
Hogg, James, 18
Hone, William, 82, 83, 84
Hoogstraaten, Samuel van, 25–6, 29
Horner, W. B., 98, 103
Horner, W. G., 35–6, 44, 127
Hughes, W. G., 93, 94, 103

I

Iamblichus, 13
Irving, 30

J

Jacob, Georg, 52, 53, 67
Jansche, 33
Jeanne, Paul, 73
Jones, Inigo, 67
Jonson, Ben, 11, 12, 67–8

K

Kaaz, 33

Keller, Heinrich, 27
Kinetoscope, 132, 134
Kinora, 134, 135
Kircher, Athanasius, 18, 19, 31, 45, 58
Kücük Ali, 64

L

Lan Hsaio-shan, 50
Lancaster's shutter, 95
Landseer, 90
Langlois, Col. J. C., 42, 43–5, 74
Le Feuvre, Amy, 104
Le Gray, G., 113
Leech, 90
Lempereur, Edmond, 77
Lever slides, 87
Li-Hsiang, 50
Lincoln, W. E., 127
Loutherbourg, Philip de, 28–31, 32, 40, 42,
  50
Lui Chen-yin, 50
Lumière Brothers, 133

M

Macklin, Jim, 78
Magic lantern, 18–21, 45, 74, 81–99
Manos, Konstantin, 64
Marey, 131
Margraf, 24–5
Marshall, Charles, 35
Martineau, Harriet, 19, 21
Mayall, J. J. E., 102
Mayhew, 78, 79, 84, 106
Meliès, 102, 134
Menucci, 69
Metamorphoser, 95

Metivet, Lucien, 77
Mirrors: Chinese, 13–14; concave, 14–15;
  cylindrical, 19, 45
Mollas, 64
Moreck, Curt, 58
Morgan, James, 38
Morin, Louis, 74
Morley, Henry, 68
Motions, 11, 68, 82
Mouchet, Jaan, 34
Mutoscope, 134, 135
Muybridge, E., 131, 132

N

Nash, John, 38
Nausorama, 32, 33
Neuville, 45
Noakes, D. W., 96–9, 101
Noakes, Ernest, 97
Noakesoscope, 97–9

O

Obraztsov, 50
Ombres chinoises, 67–80

P

Panorama, 28, 31, 32–5, 43, 46, 74
Panoramic slides, 83–6
Paris, John Ayrton, 122–3
Parke, W. D., 29
Peep-eggs, 27
Peepshows, 23–8
Penkethman, William, 28
Phantasmagoria, 19–21, 43, 69, 71

Phenakistiscope, 125–6
Philippoteaux, 45
Philipsthal, M., 20–1, 69
Plateau, J. A. F., 124–6
Pleuorama, 43
Pliny the Elder, 13
Pollonais, Gaston, 77
Porta, Giacomo della, 23
Postle, 33
Praxinoscope, 128
Praxinoscope Theatre, 128–9
Prévost, Pierre, 34, 35, 36, 43
Projected Praxinoscope, 129
Projecting Phenakistiscope, 127, 130, 132
Pugin, A. C., 38
Pulley slides, 88

Q

Qaraqusch, 59

R

Rack-work slides, 87–8
Rejlander, O. G., 113
Reiniger, Lotte, 80
Renoux, C. C., 39, 40
Reynaud, Emile, 128
Riley Brothers, 103, 117
Ritter, Hellmut, 64
Rivière, Henri, 73, 74–6, 77
Roberts, David, 31, 46
Robertson, 21
Robinson, H. P., 113
Rudge Projector, 130, 132

S

Sala, George, 46

Salis, Rudolphe, 72, 73, 77
Sanger, James, 28
Schinkel, C. F., 42
Seraphin, Dominique, 70–1, 78
Shadow shows: Chinese, 48–51; Greek, 64; Indian, 52–3, 58; Japanese, 51–2; Javanese, 54–7; Siamese, 53–4; Turkish, 59–65
Shadra Film Company, 58
Silvry, C., 113
Sims, George R., 104–5, 128
Slipping slides, 86–7
Somm, Henry, 73
Stampfer, S., 125
Stanfield, Clarkson, 31, 44, 46
Steinlein, 77
Stratton, Hesba, 104
Stratton, Mercy, 104
Stroboscope, 125
Sun Kai-ti, 48

T

Tachyscope, 129
Terpuoscope, 95
Thaumatrope, 122–4
Thayer, James, 34, 35
Thévenor, 59
Tinchant, Albert, 74
Trombert, F., 77

U

Uchatius, Franz, 126–7

V

Vignola, 76
Viviscope, 129

INDEX

W

Walpole, Horace, 29
Walton, Mrs. O. F., 104, 116
Watt, Van de, 33
Wheel of Life, 127
Wheel of Light, 127
Wilkie, Sir David, 47

X

Xanthos, Markos, 64

Z

Zoetrope, 127–9
Zoogyroscope, 131–2